YEMEN CHEN / FRIAR HILL
2020

Friar Hill

Friar Hill

Carved by God

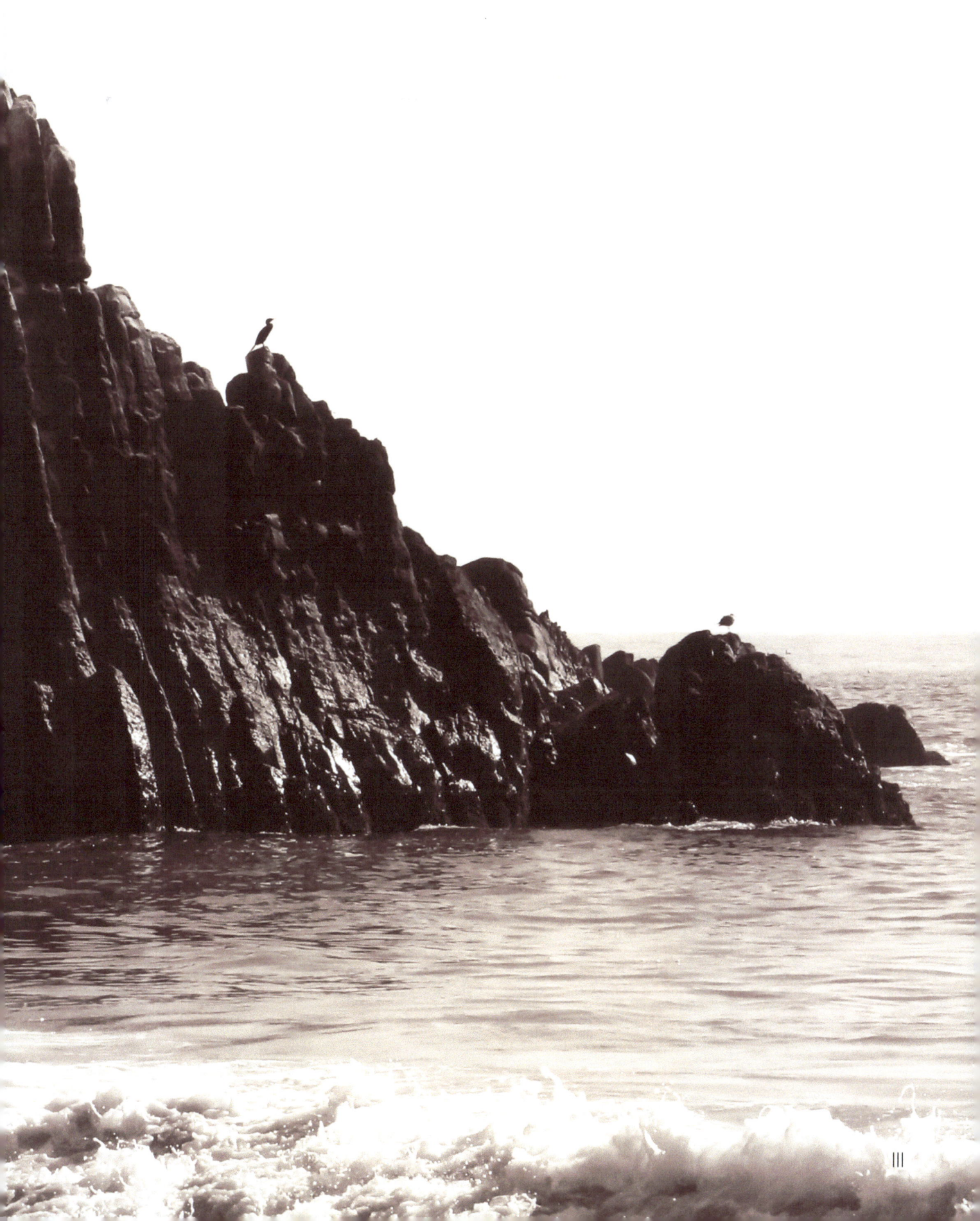

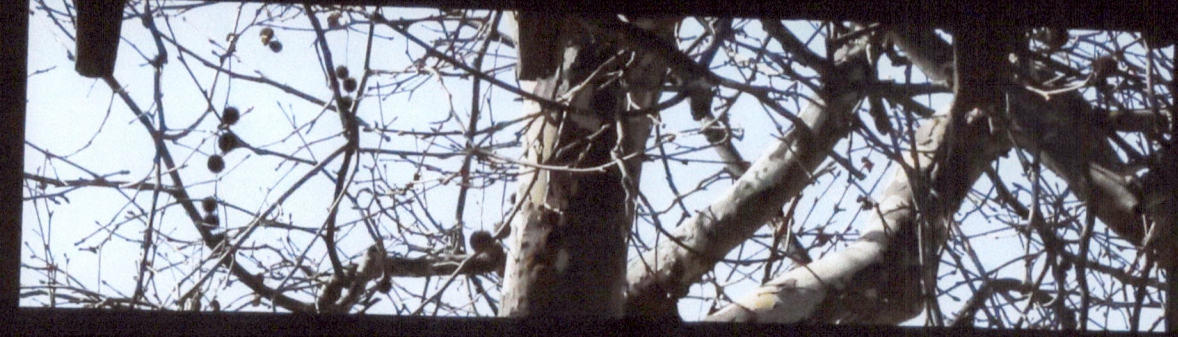

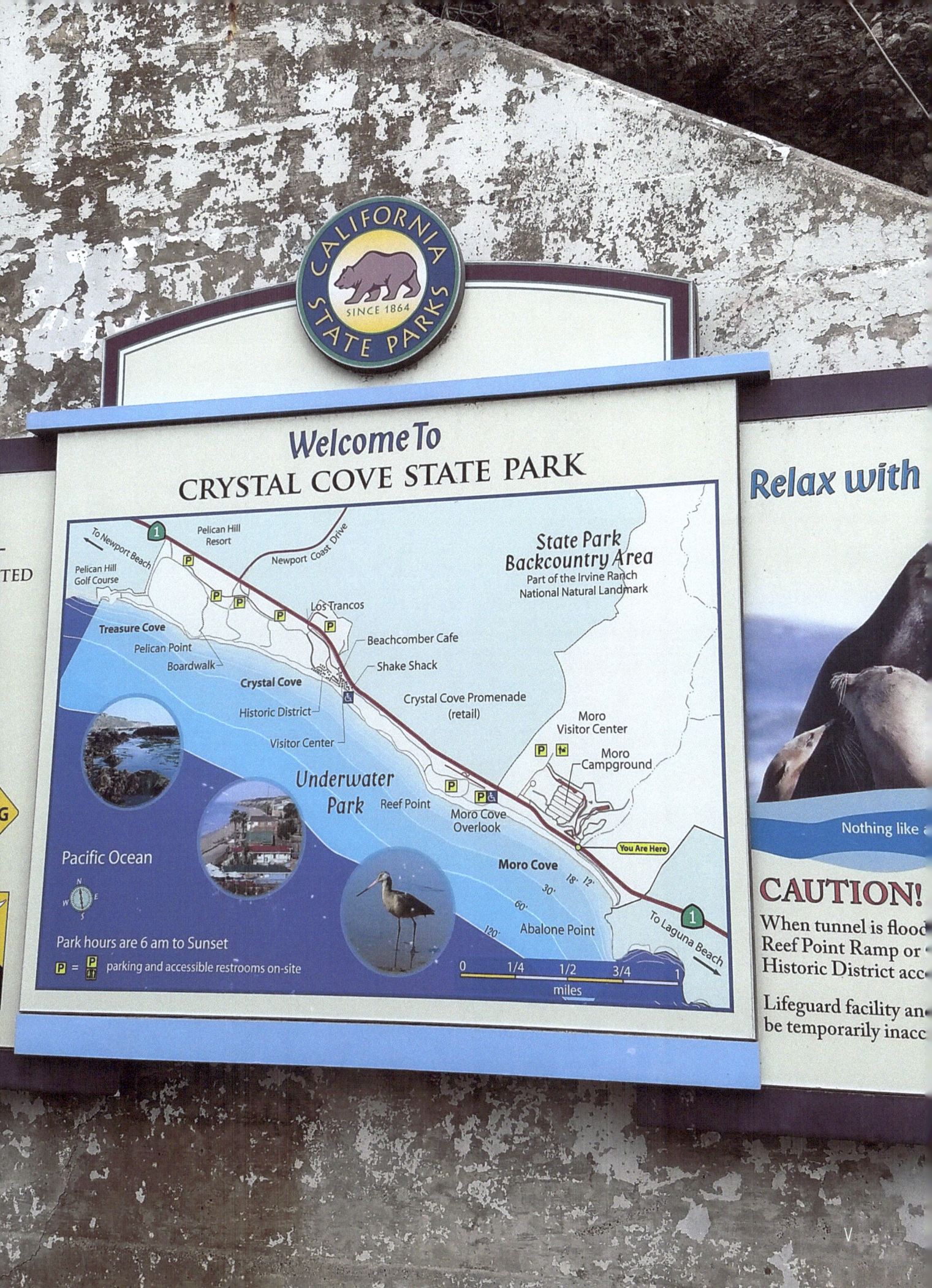

Friar Hill

Author: Yemen Chen
Photography by Yemen Chen
Editor: Darwin Alden
Author Portrait by Jane Yu

LOSGET

Copyright © 2020 by Yemen Chen
All rights reserved.
Published in the United States by Losget Press, Los Angeles
Originally published in Paperback in the United States by Losget Press, in 2020
Title: Friar Hill
Description: First Edition. | Los Angeles: Losget Press, 2020.
Identifiers: ISBN-13: 978-1-951364-01-4 | ISBN-10: 1-951364-01-5 | Library of Congress Control Number (LCCN): 2020934623
www.losget.com
E-mail: contact@losget.com
Book design by Yemen Chen
First Printing. 2020.

1st Edition

Friar Cliff - Carved by God

Friar Hill

Author: Yemen Chen
Photography by Yemen Chen
Editor: Darwin Alden
Author Portrait by Jane Yu
Cover and Interior Design by Yemen Chen

LOSGET
Losget Press
2020

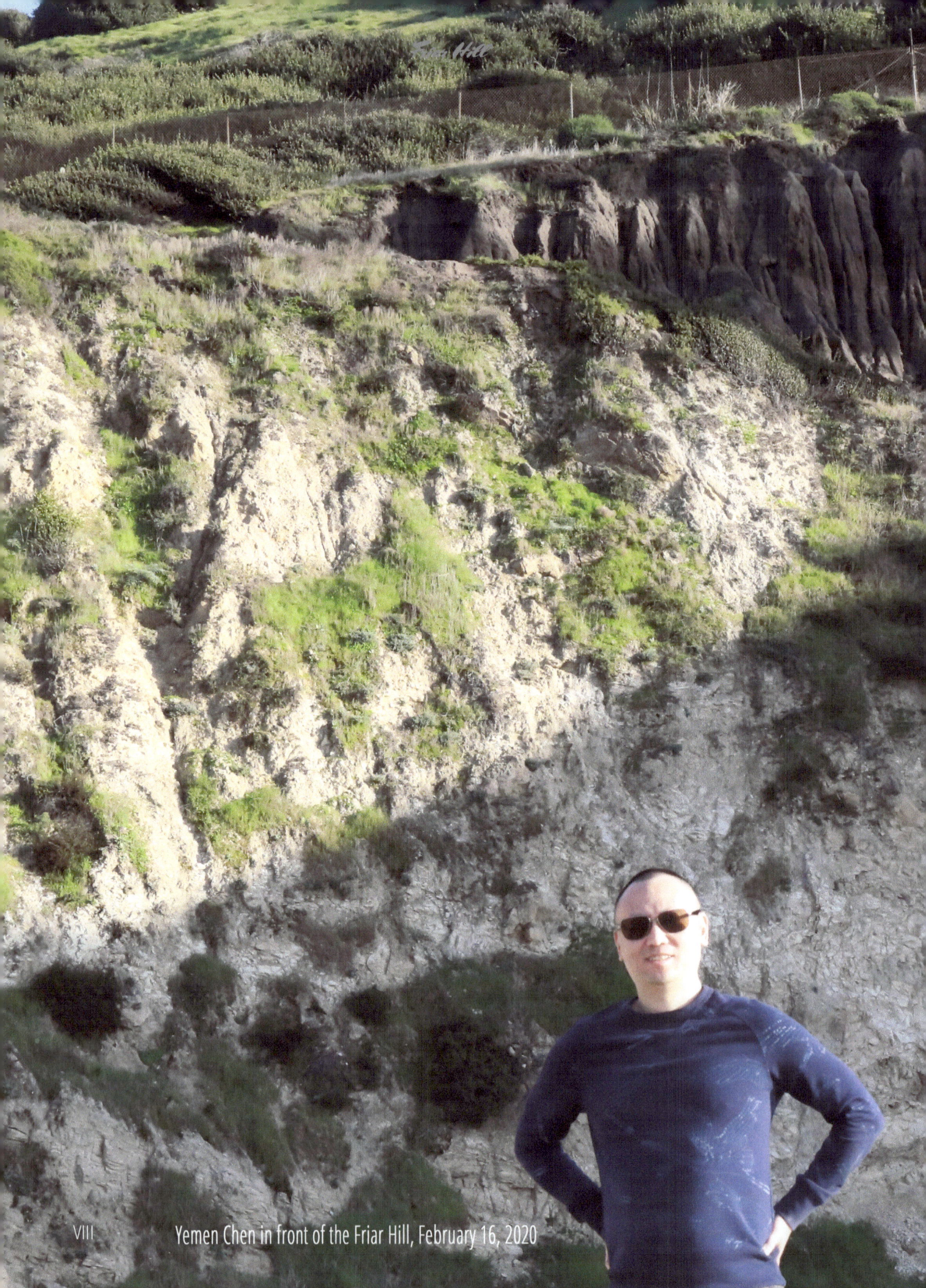

VIII Yemen Chen in front of the Friar Hill, February 16, 2020

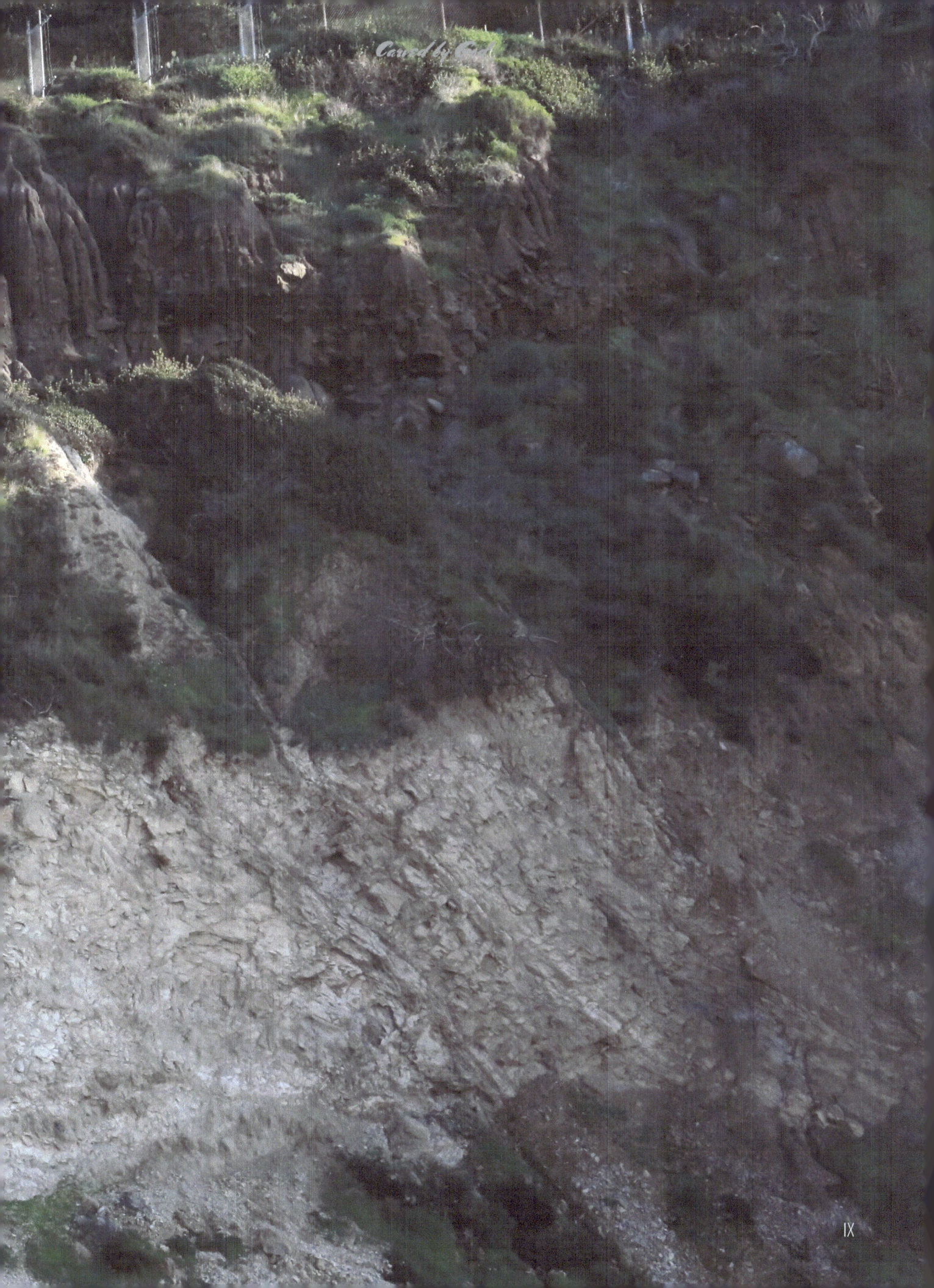
Carved by God

IX

CONTENTS

History.........................1
Geography....................2
Friar Hill......................3
Friars in Famous Paintings......27
Yemen Chen.....................36
Yemen Chen.....................37
Online Bookselling................38
Font Description.....................39
Publishing Information...........40

HISTORY

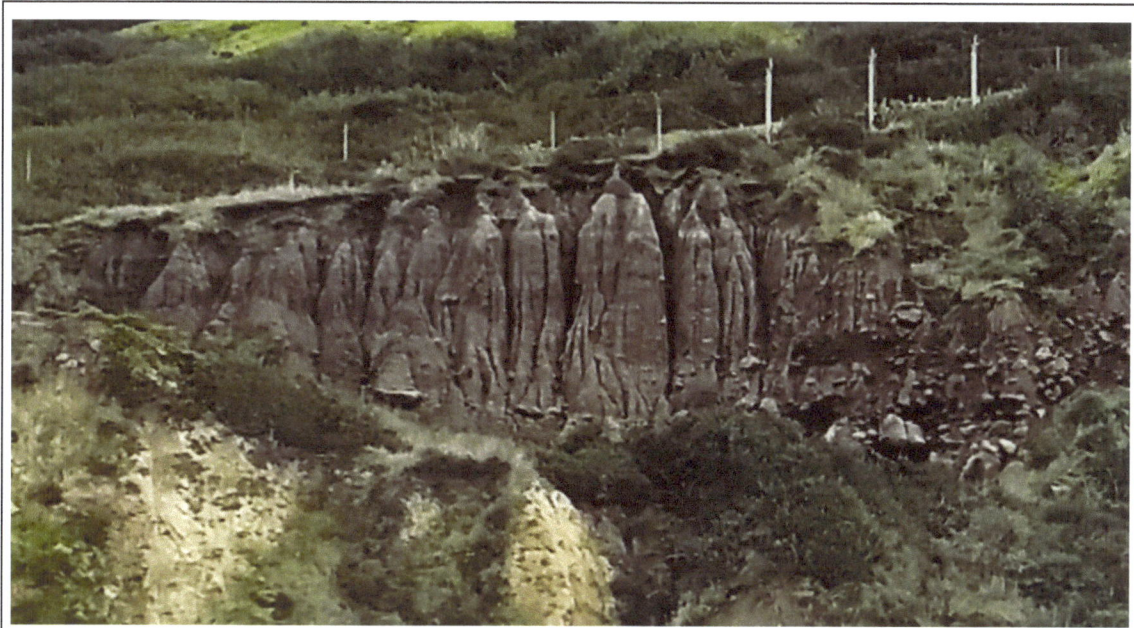

Picture 1: This photo was taken by Yemen Chen on January 19, 2020 with his smartphone. Because it was cloudy, the images of those friars are in vividness.

On January 19, 2020, it was cloudy. Artist Yemen Chen came to Moro Beach for a hike; it was his first time here.

Moro Beach is the southern beach in Crystal Cove State Park located between Laguna Beach and the Corona Del Mar area of Newport Beach, California, USA.

The sea was beating on the beach, and a hill on the beach extended into the Pacific Ocean. When Yemen Chen was close to this hill, he found a naturally formed "relief" on this hill's cliff, which looked like a group of friars marching in the air. Yemen Chen could not find the hill's name on the map, then he named it "Friar Hill".

Yemen Chen took some pictures of the "Friar Relief" with his smartphone (see Figure 1). Because it was a rare cloudy day in California that day, the "Friar Relief" became apparent.

On February 16, 2020, Yemen Chen came here again with a camera. The sun was strong that day, and the friars' image seemed to disappear under intense sunlight; that place looked like an ordinary cliff (see Figure 2).

To take perfect pictures, Yemen Chen waited there for a long time. Until there was a short time when some clouds blocked the sun from shining there, the "friars" reappeared—Yemen Chen finally took some pictures that he needed.

The ideal weather to appreciate the natural relief of these friars is cloudy. However, suppose you are eager to appreciate. In that case, you can go there on any sunny day. After all, in California, it is not easy to encounter a cloudy day. As long as you sincerely wait, at a certain moment, when some shadows cover that magical part of the cliff, a sacred image would appear in front of you.

Yemen Chen referred to the natural relief of the friars on this cliff as the "relief carved by God."

Yemen Chen has created many illusion artworks, such as *The Creation, Hedgehog and Deer, Statue of Liberty*. He found that many famous images in the world hid some particular information. He believed that God was sending information in His way.

Yemen Chen is also a writer. He founded the full-rhyme and alliteration articles. He also wrote the most homonyms, full-rhymes, alliterations, and tongue twisters in the world.

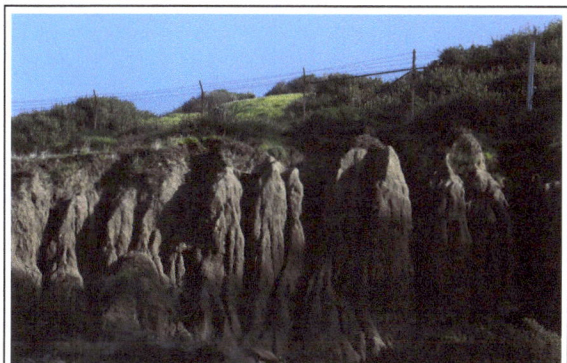

Picture 2. This photo was taken by Yemen Chen on February 16, 2020. Because of the strong sunlight at the time, the relief of the friars disappeared, and it looked like an ordinary cliff.

GEOGRAPHY

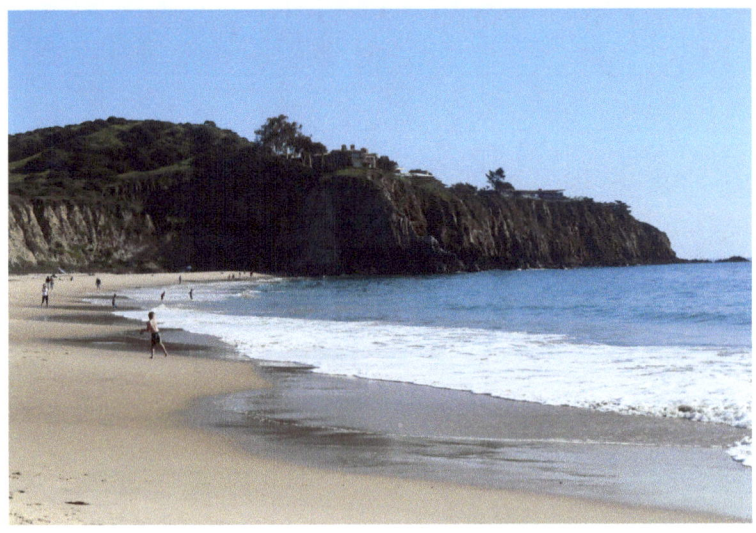

"Friar Hill", located in Moro Beach, is a naturally formed cliff with vivid friar relief, which were discovered by an artist Yemen Chen on January 19, 2020.

Moro Beach is the southern beach in Crystal Cove State Park, which lies in a coastal city Newport Beach, CA, USA.

Friar Hill

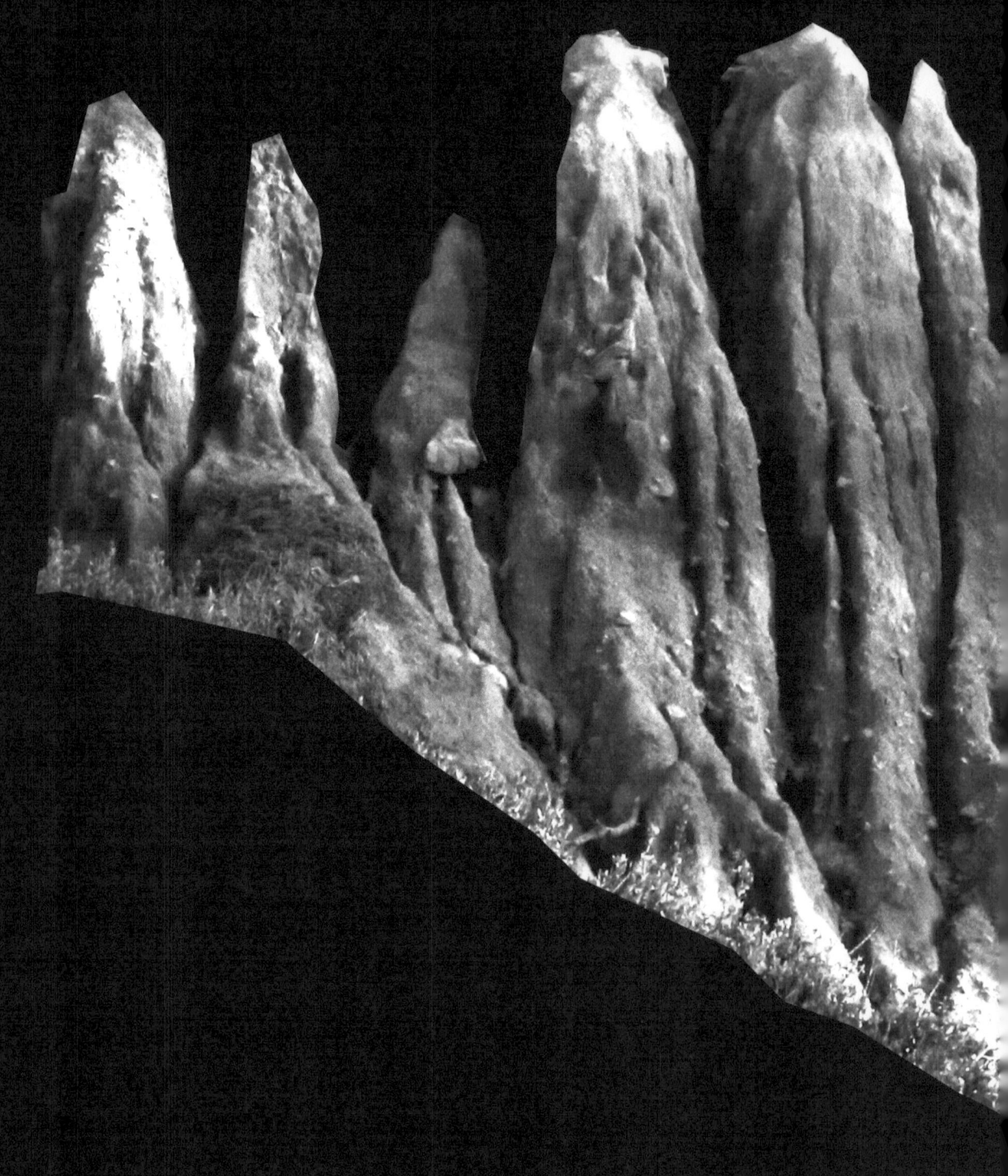

Friar Hill

Carved by God

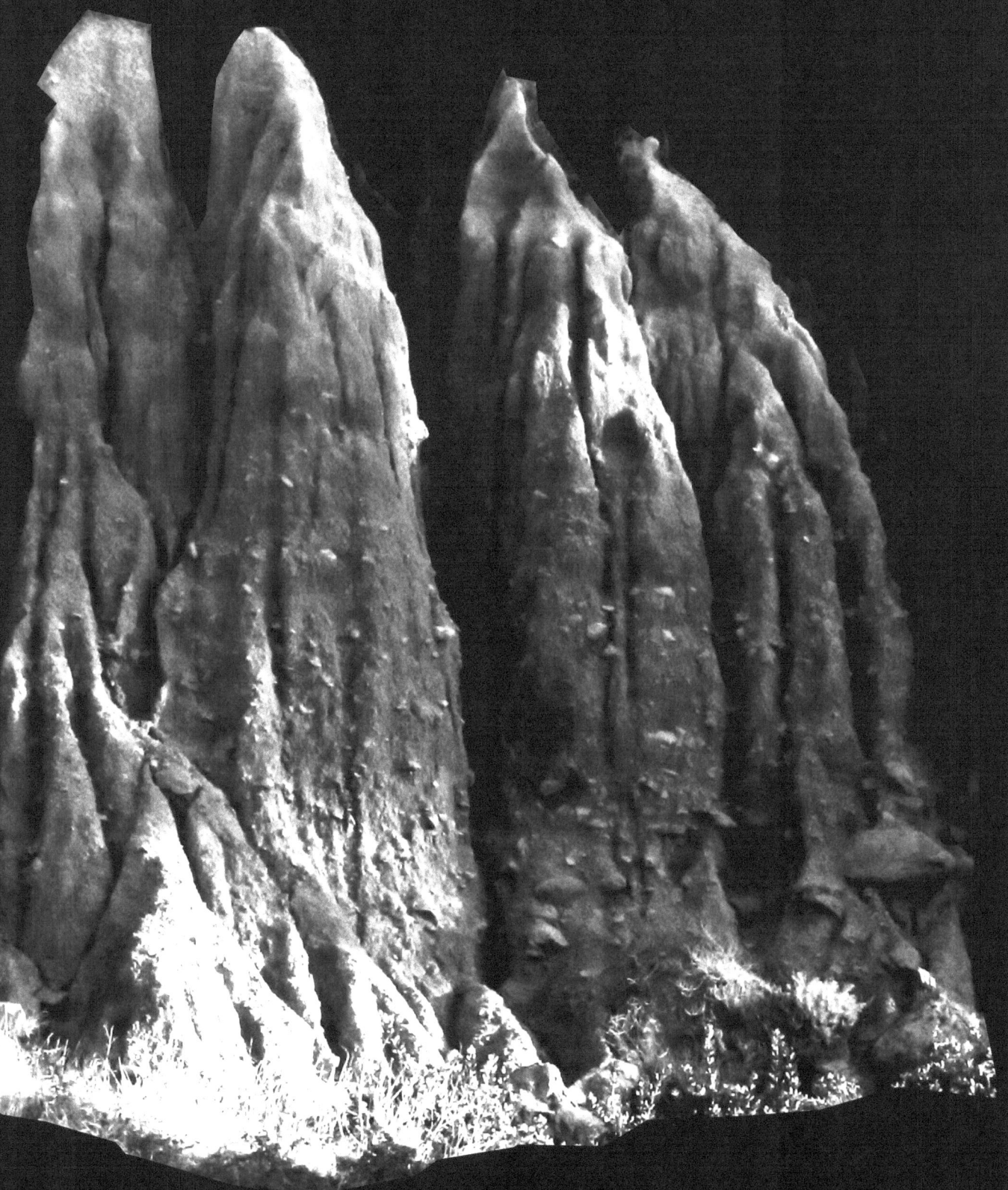

Friar Hill

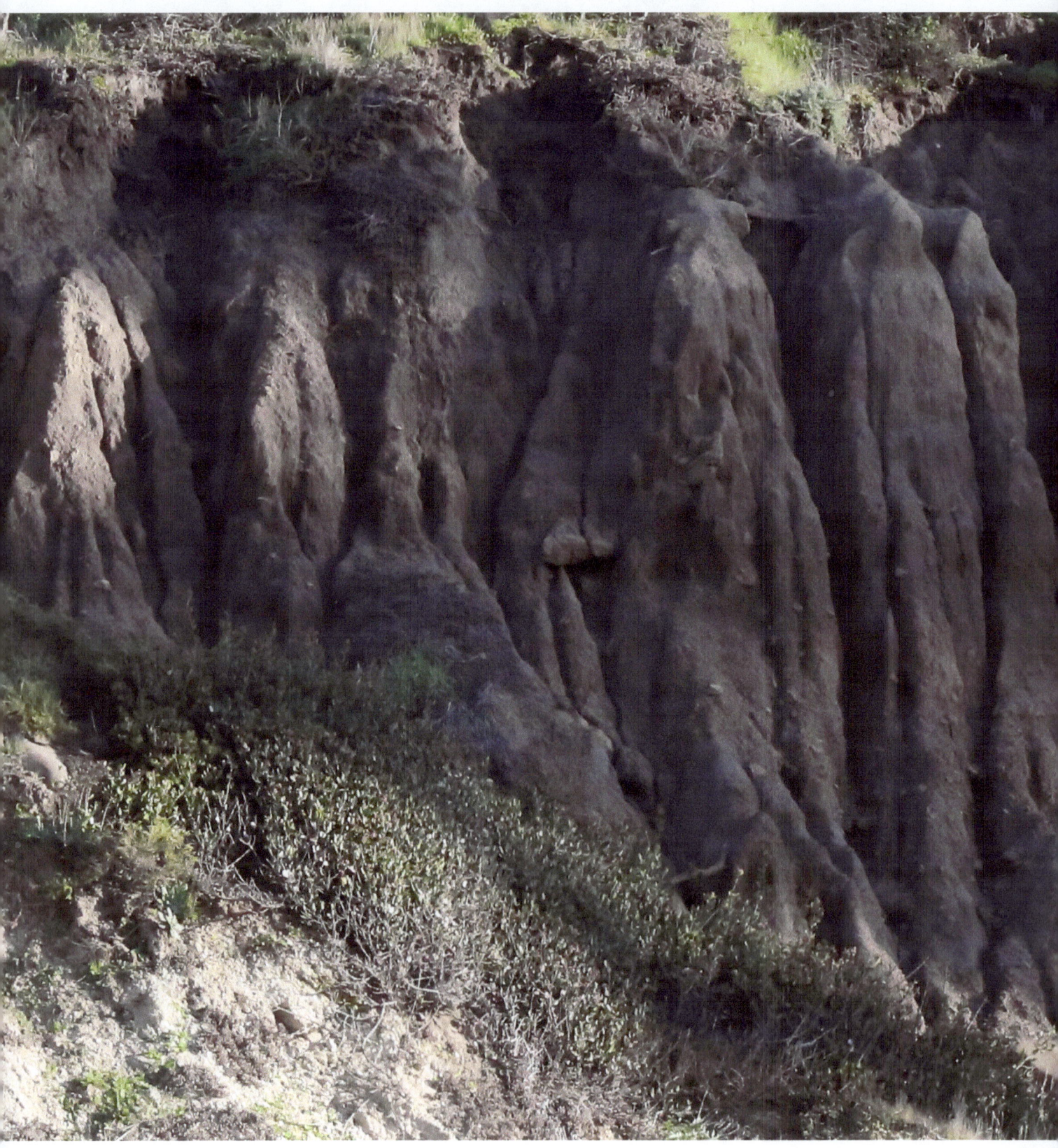

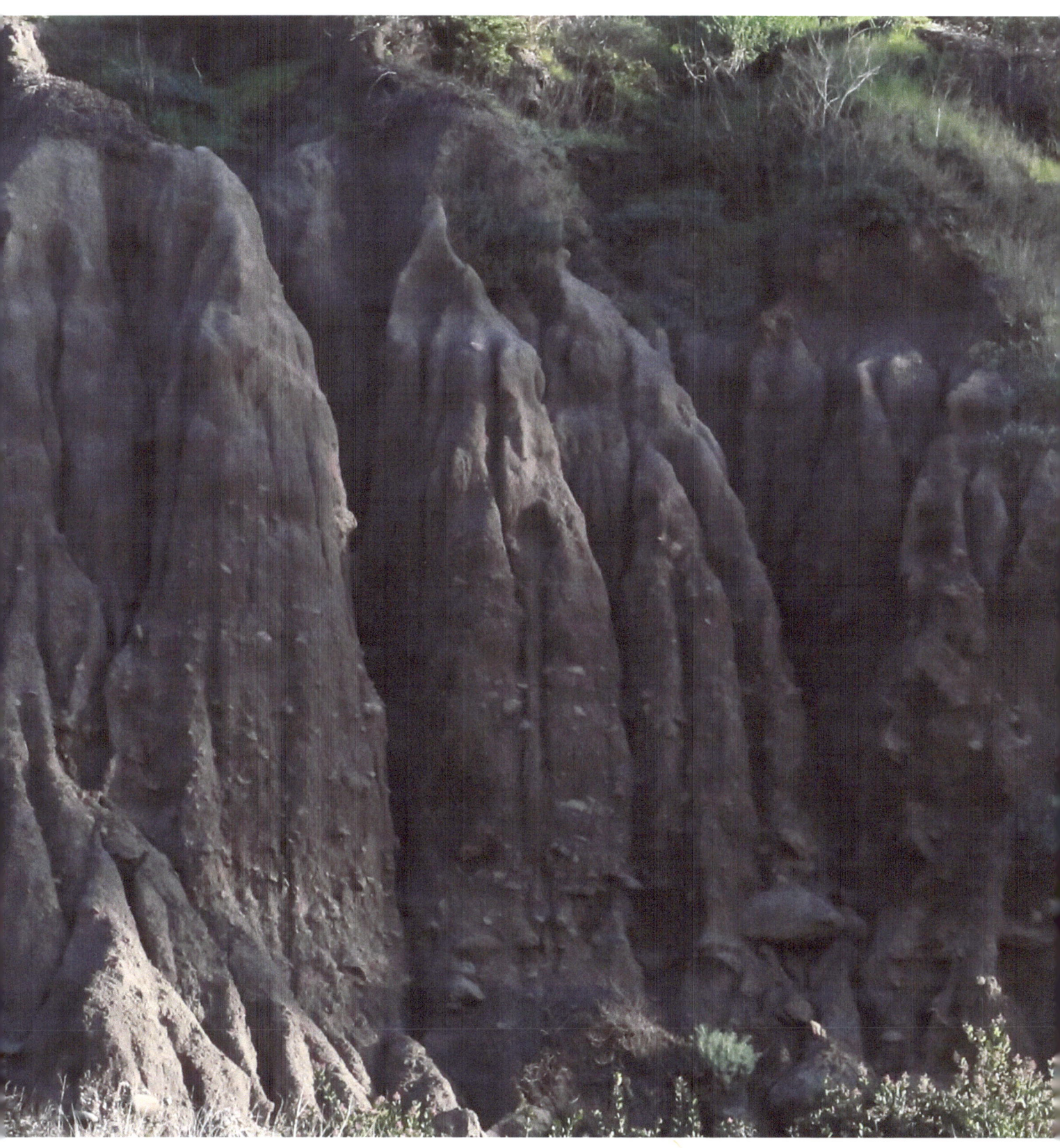

Friar Hill

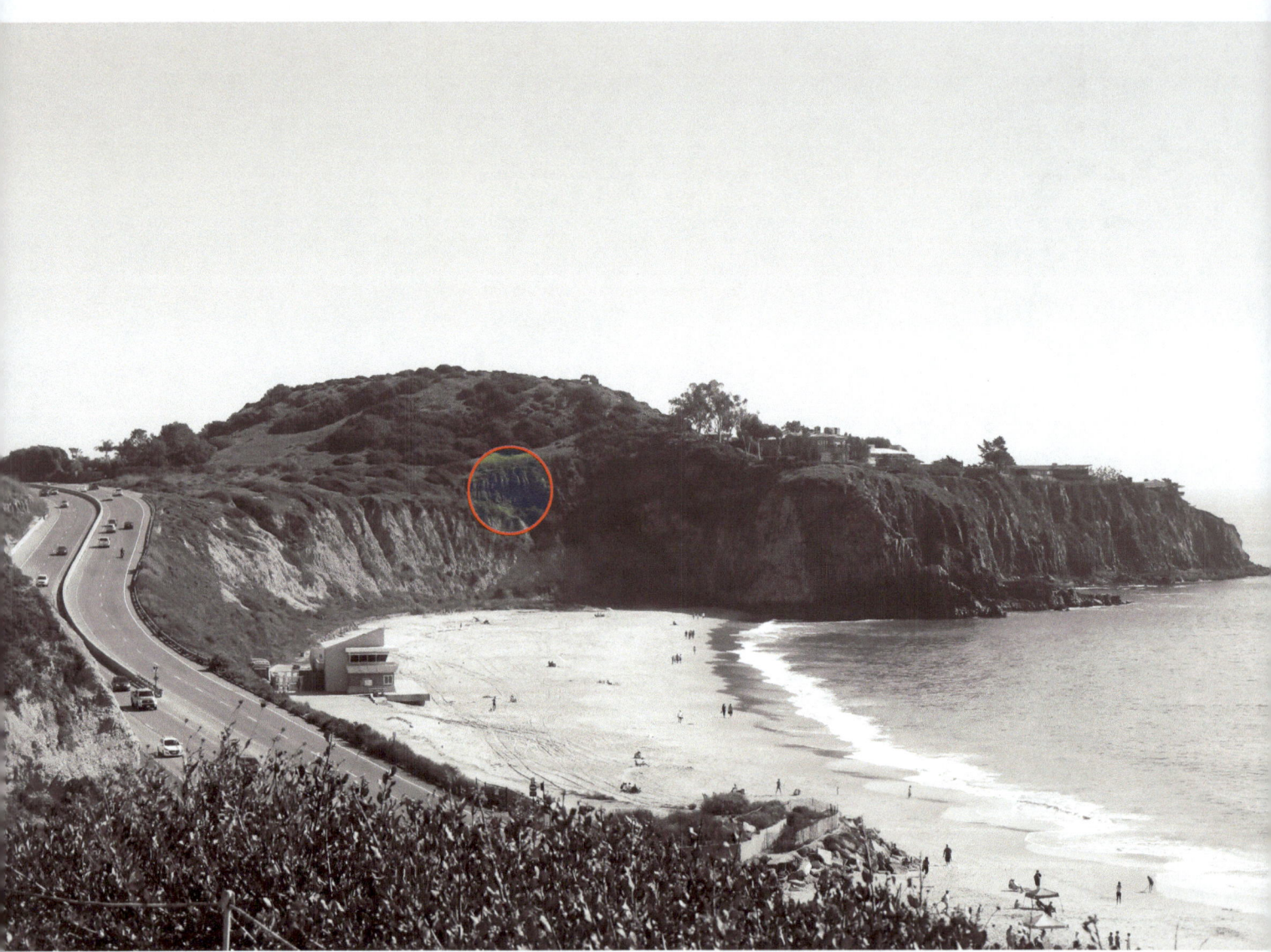

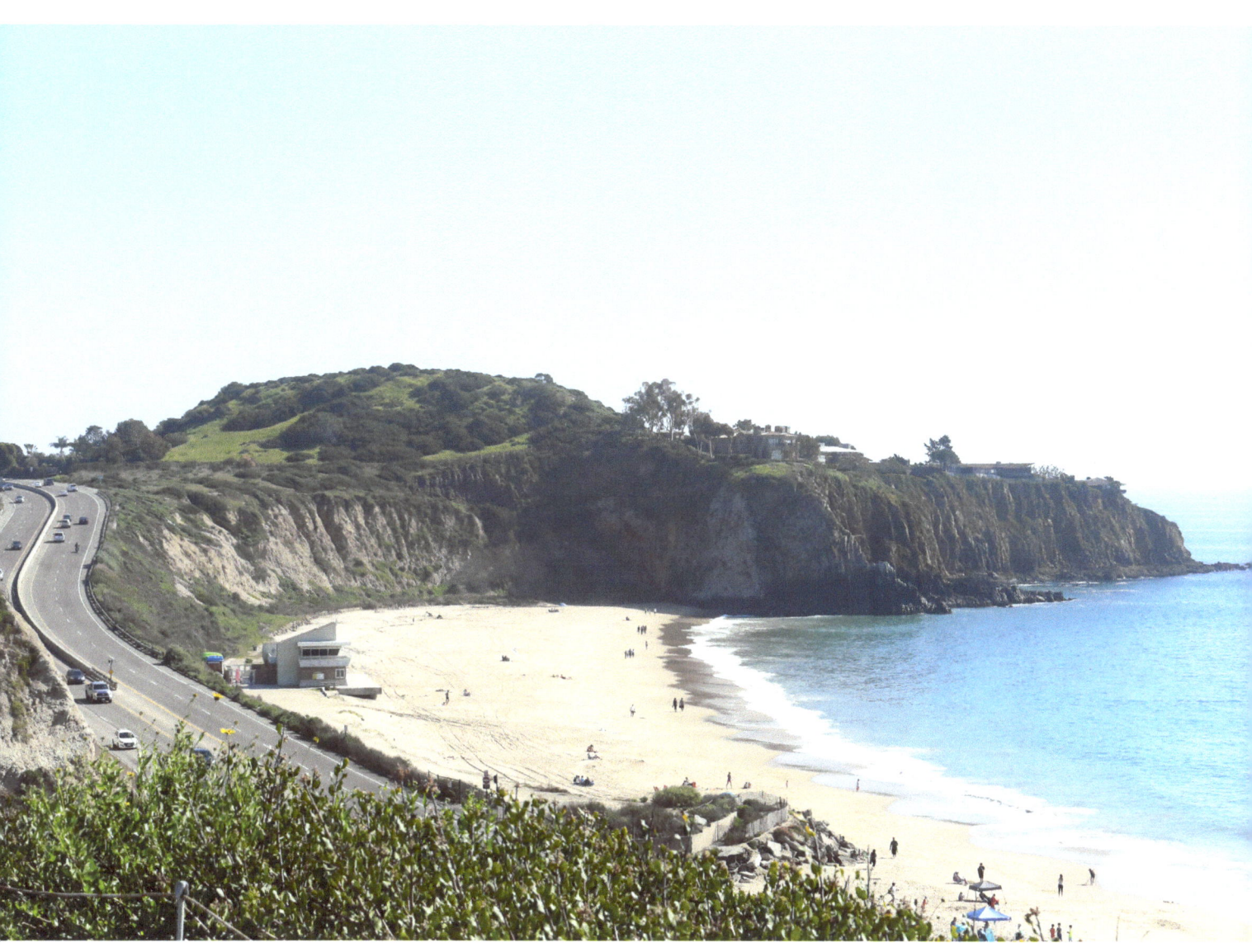

Friar Hill

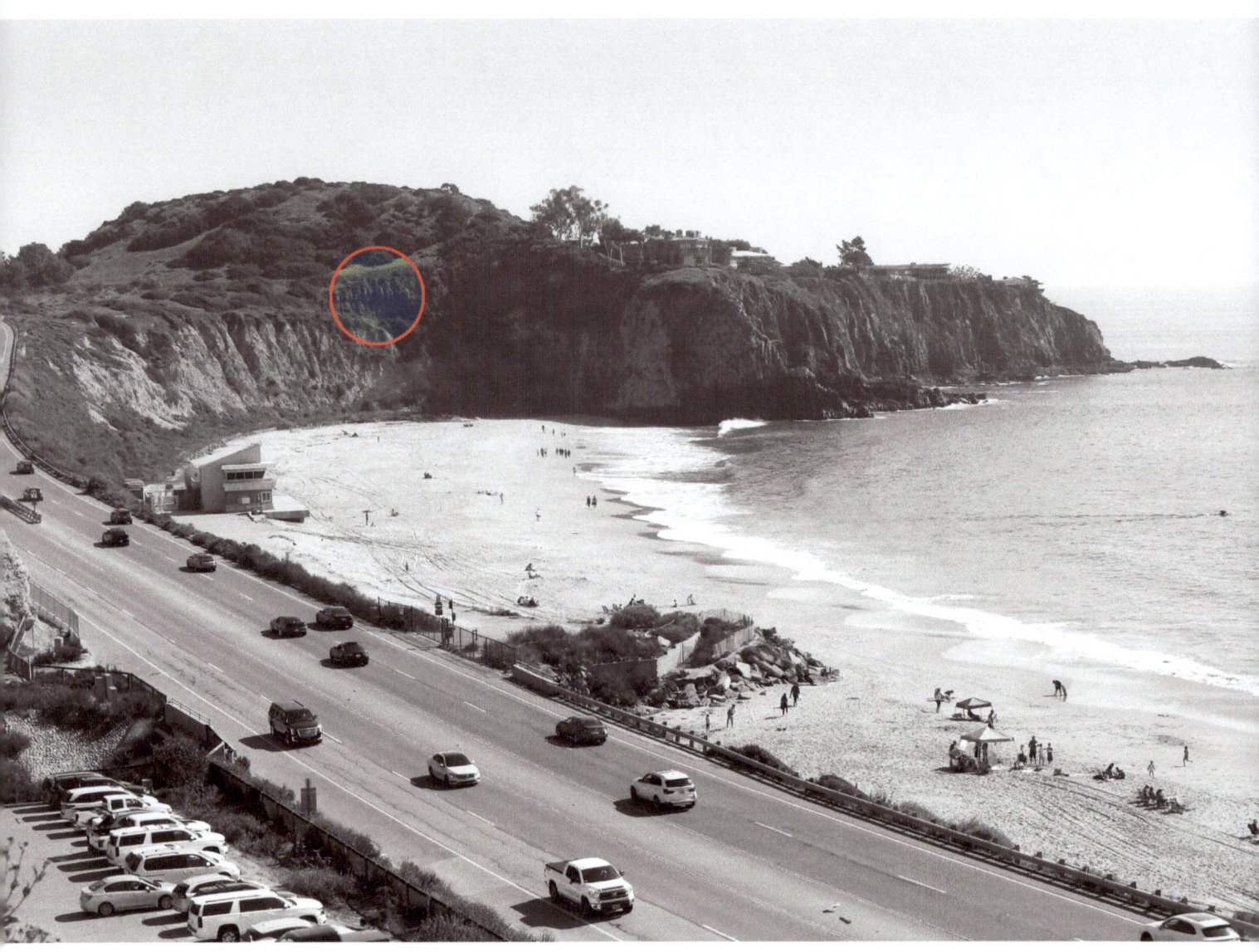

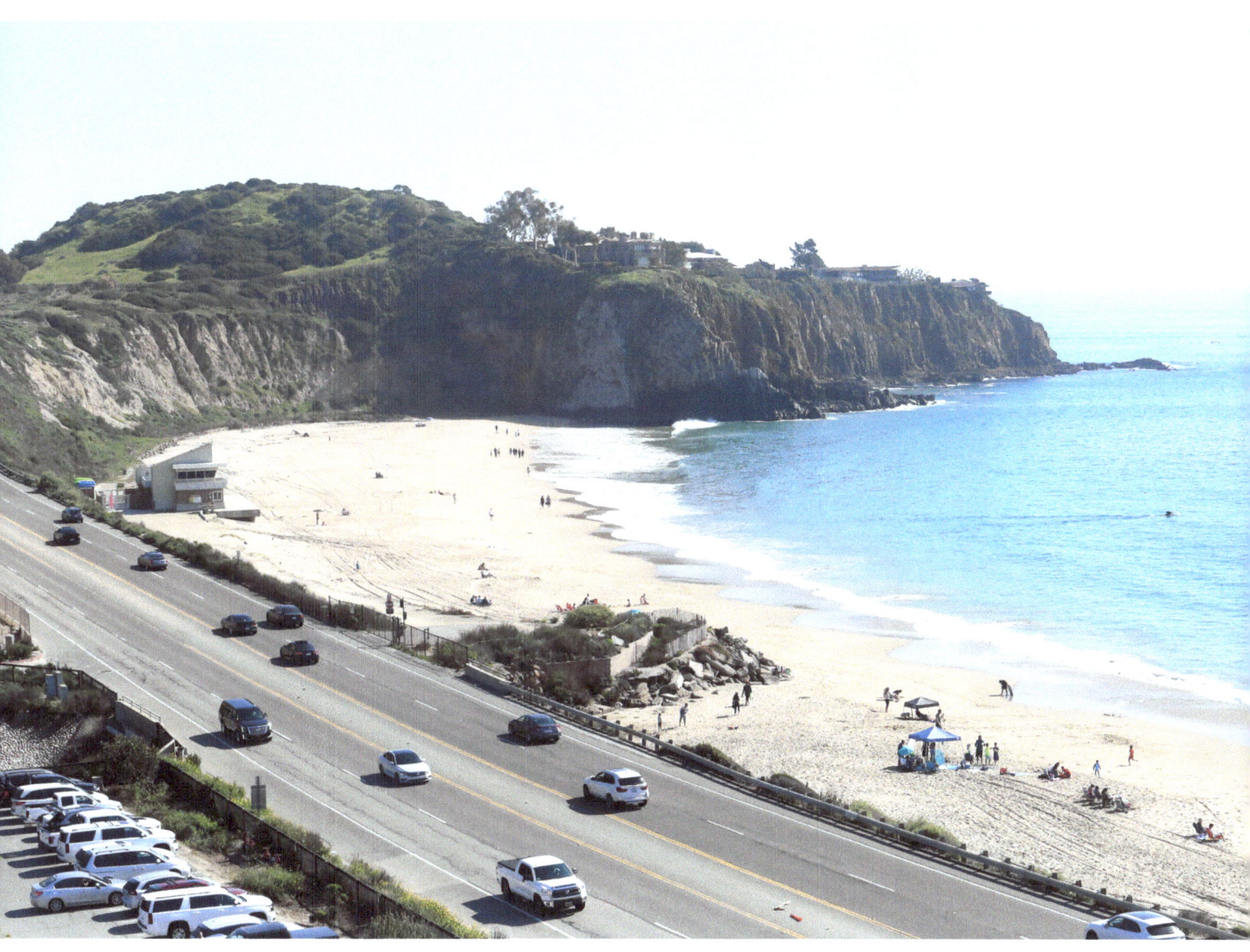

Friar Hill

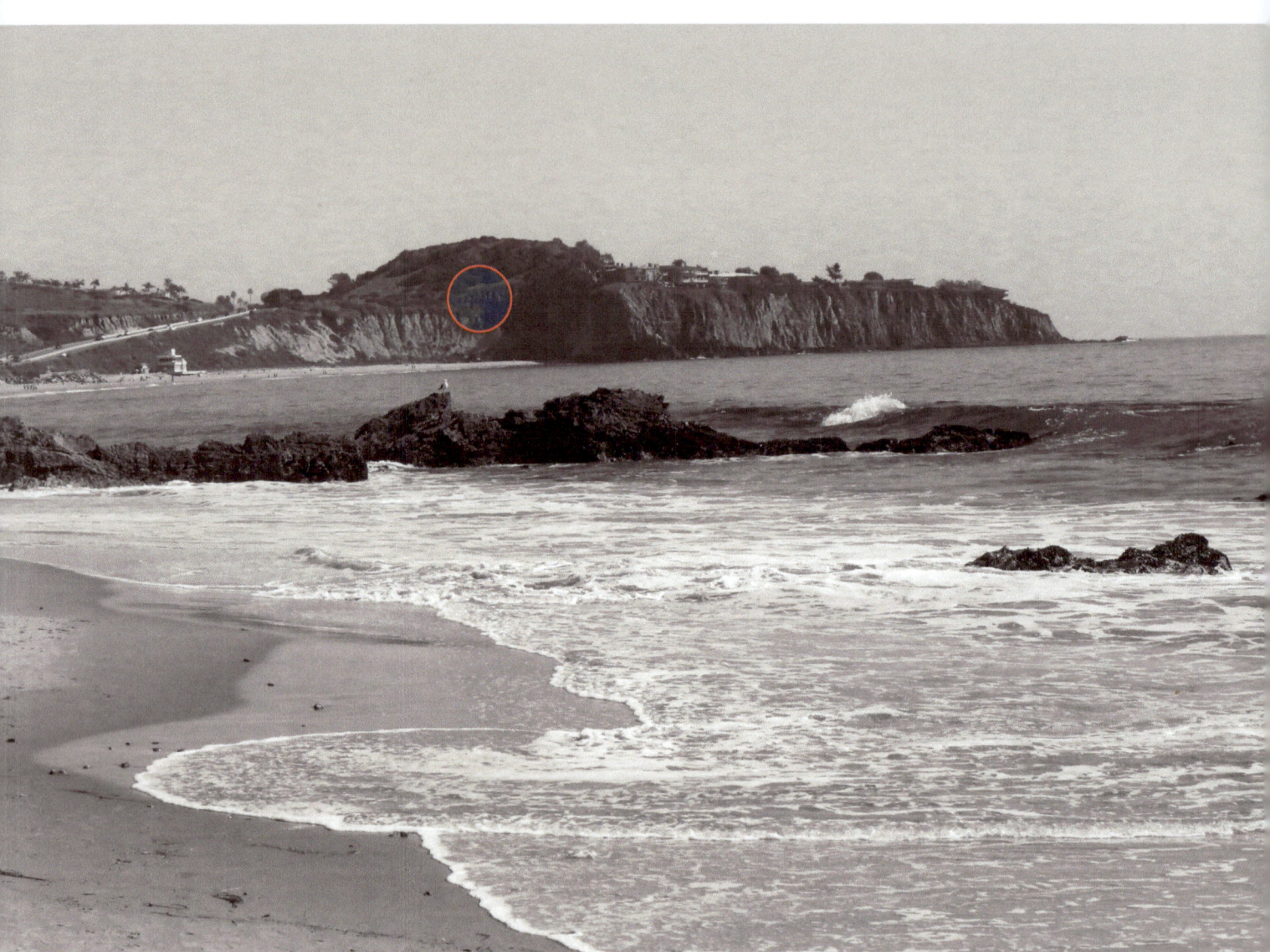

Friar Hill

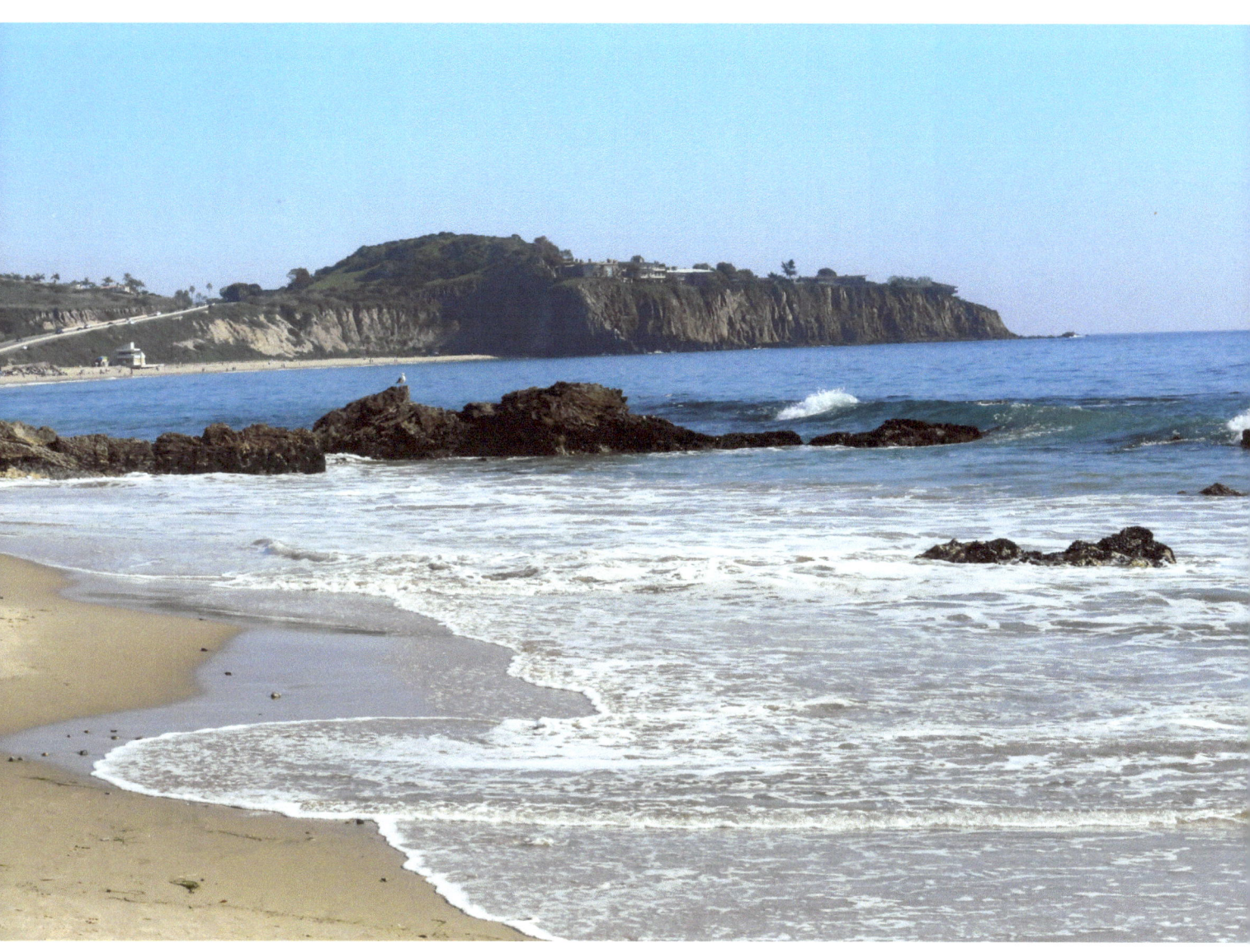

Friar Hill

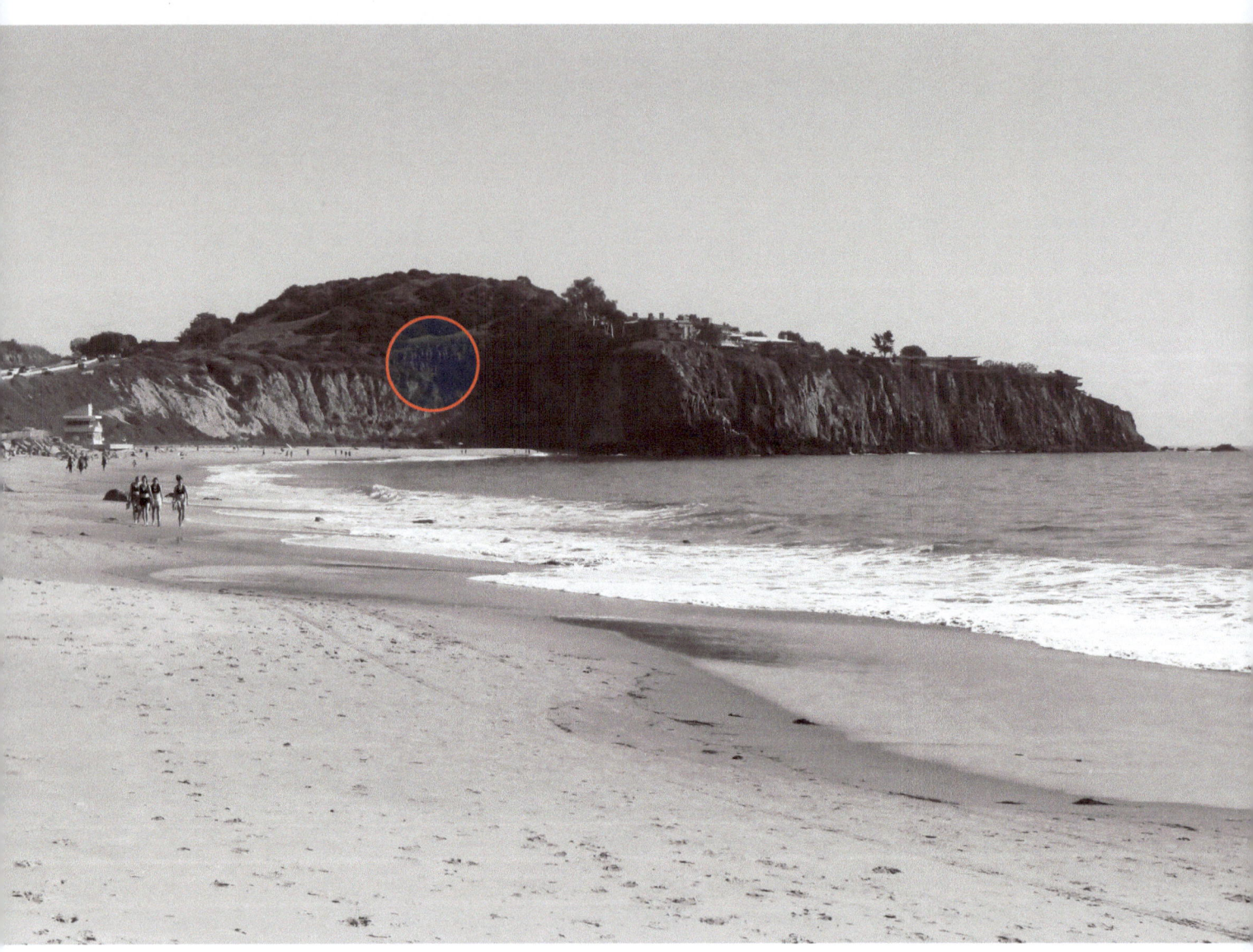

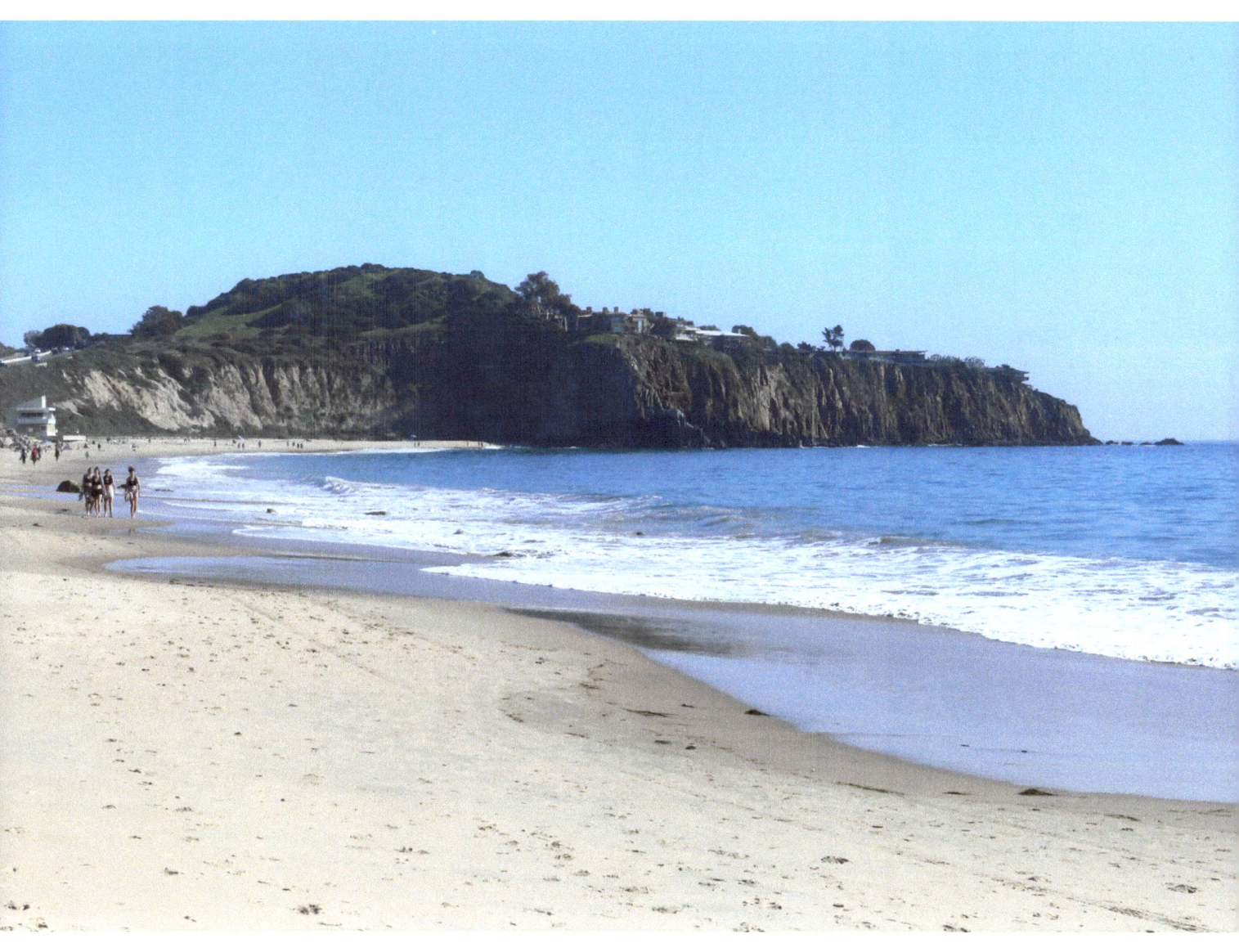

Friar Hill

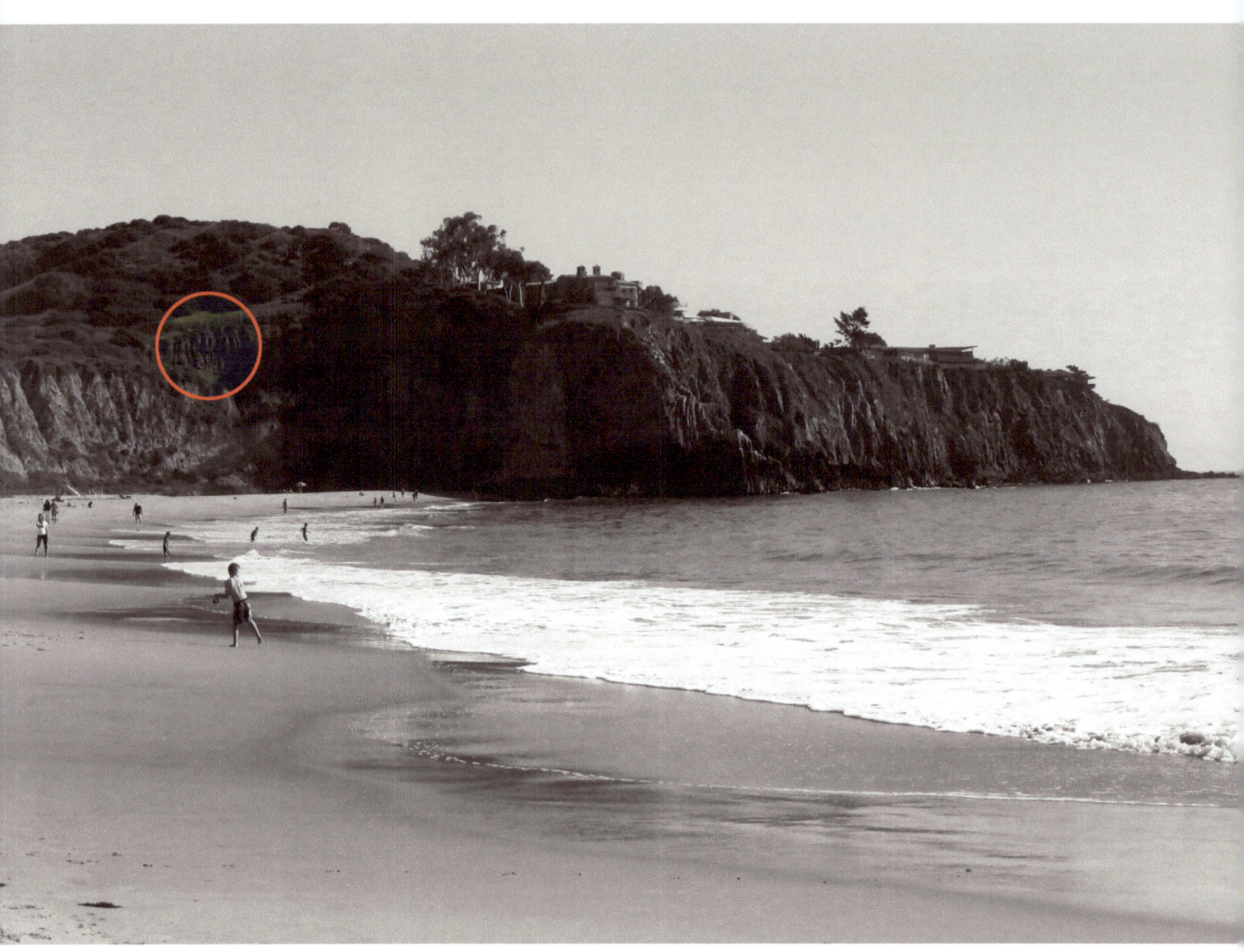

Friar Hill

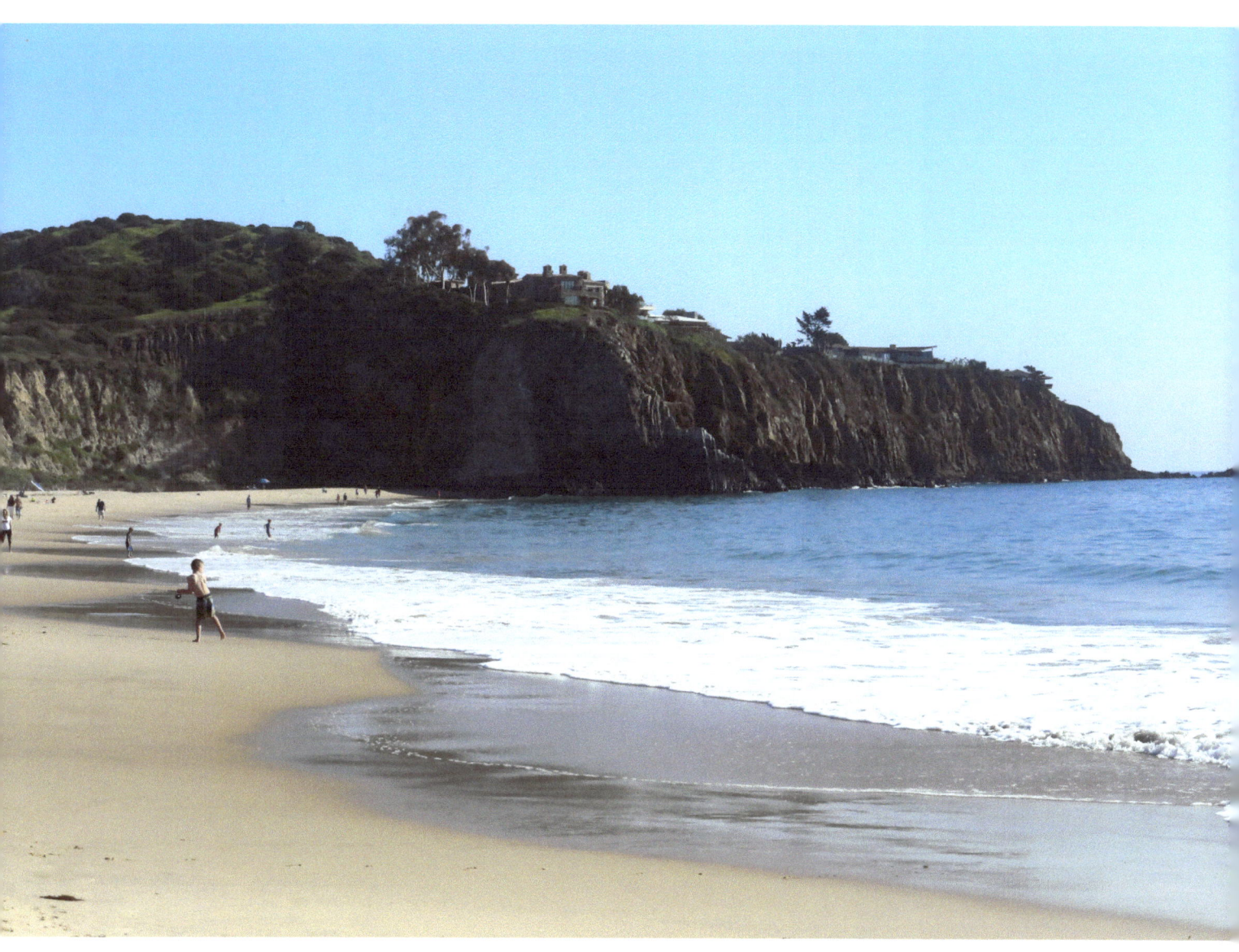

Friar Hill

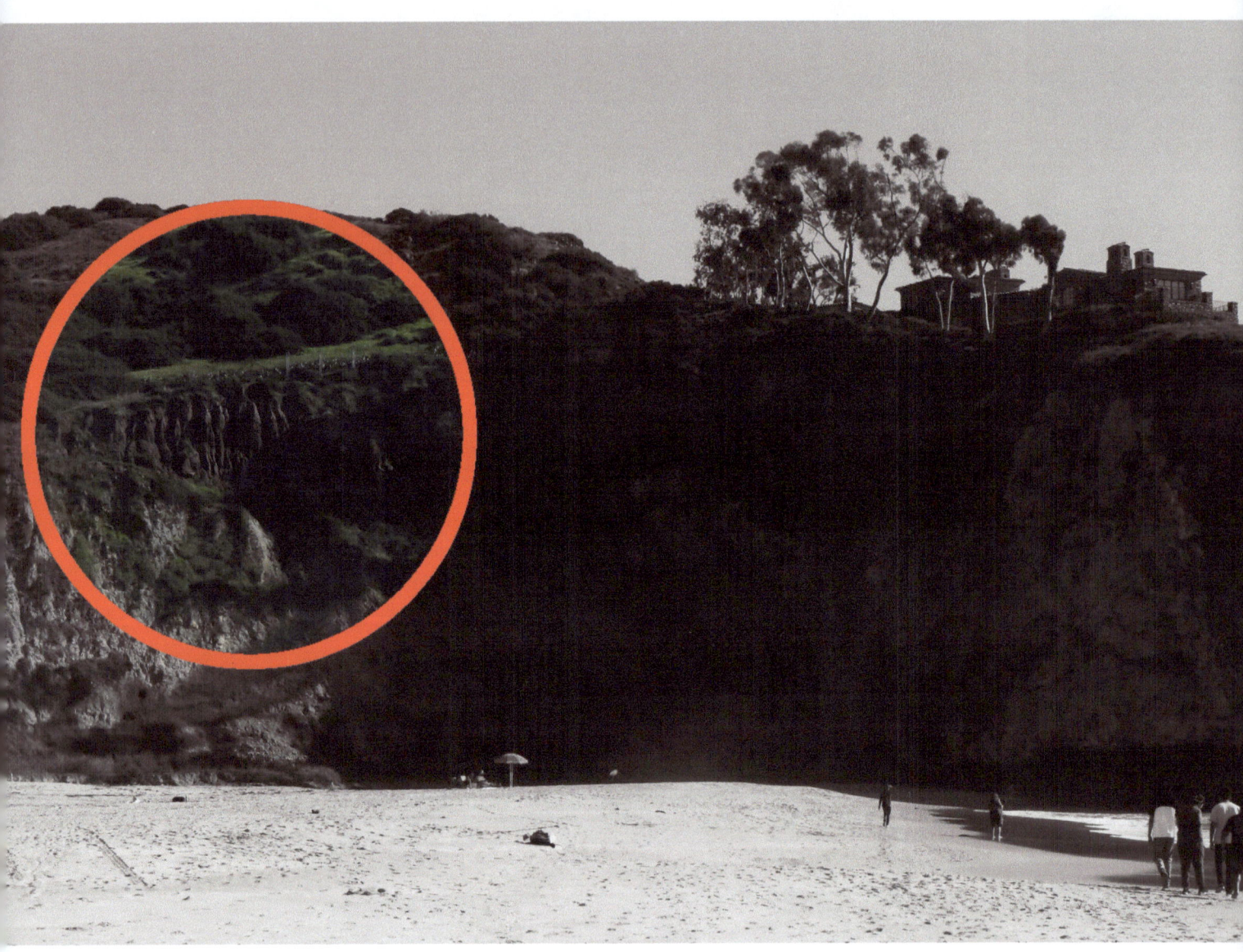

Carved by God

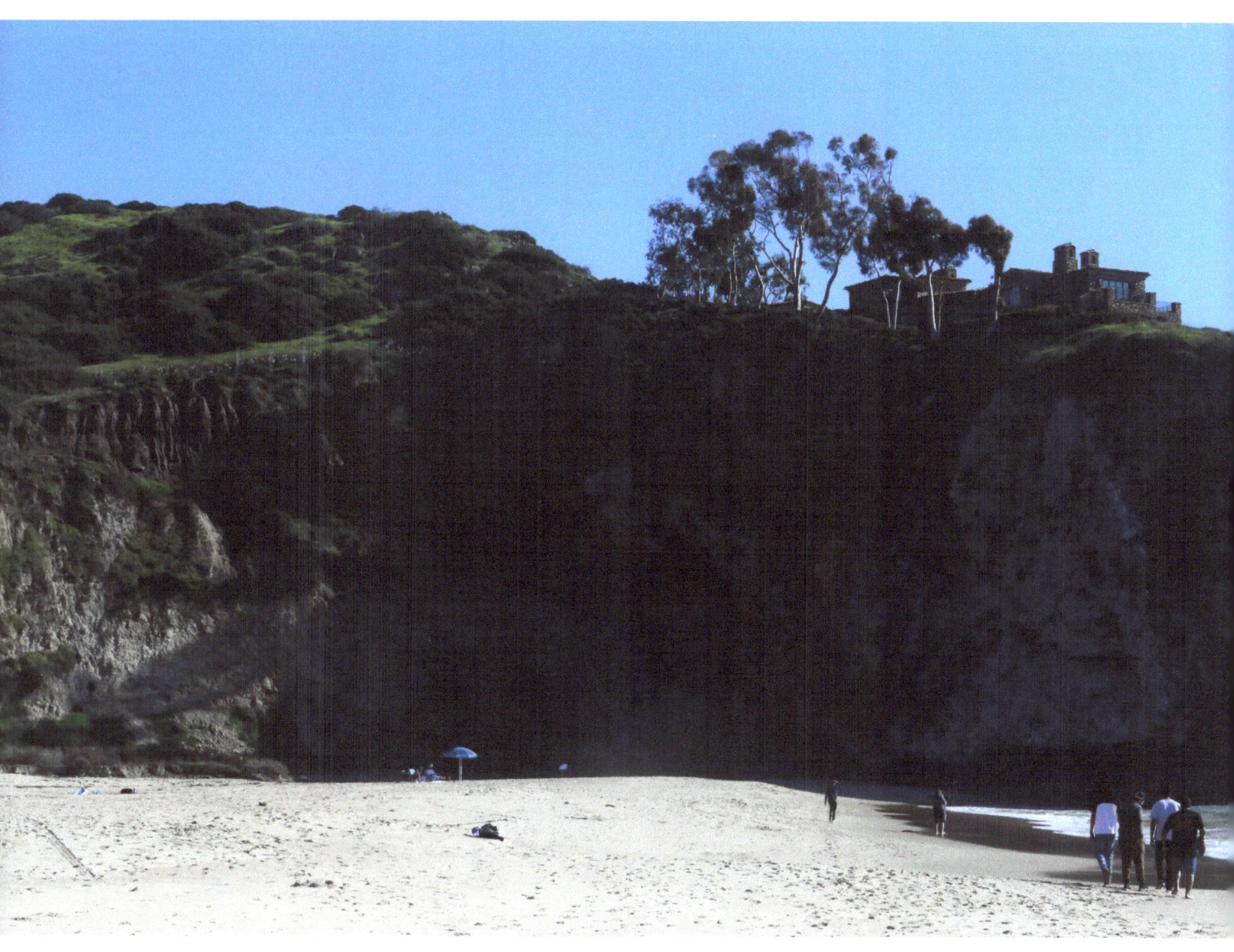

Friar Hill

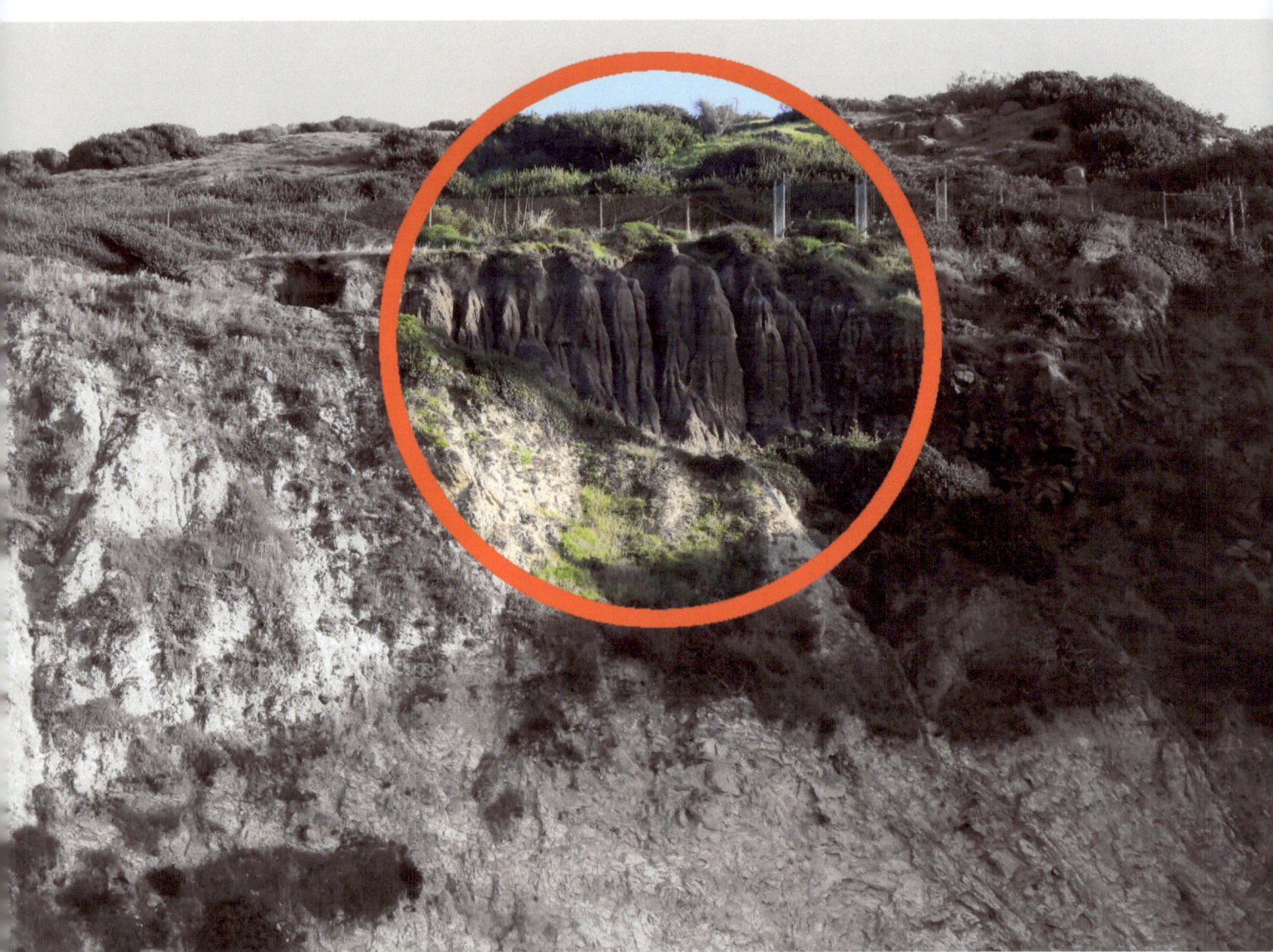

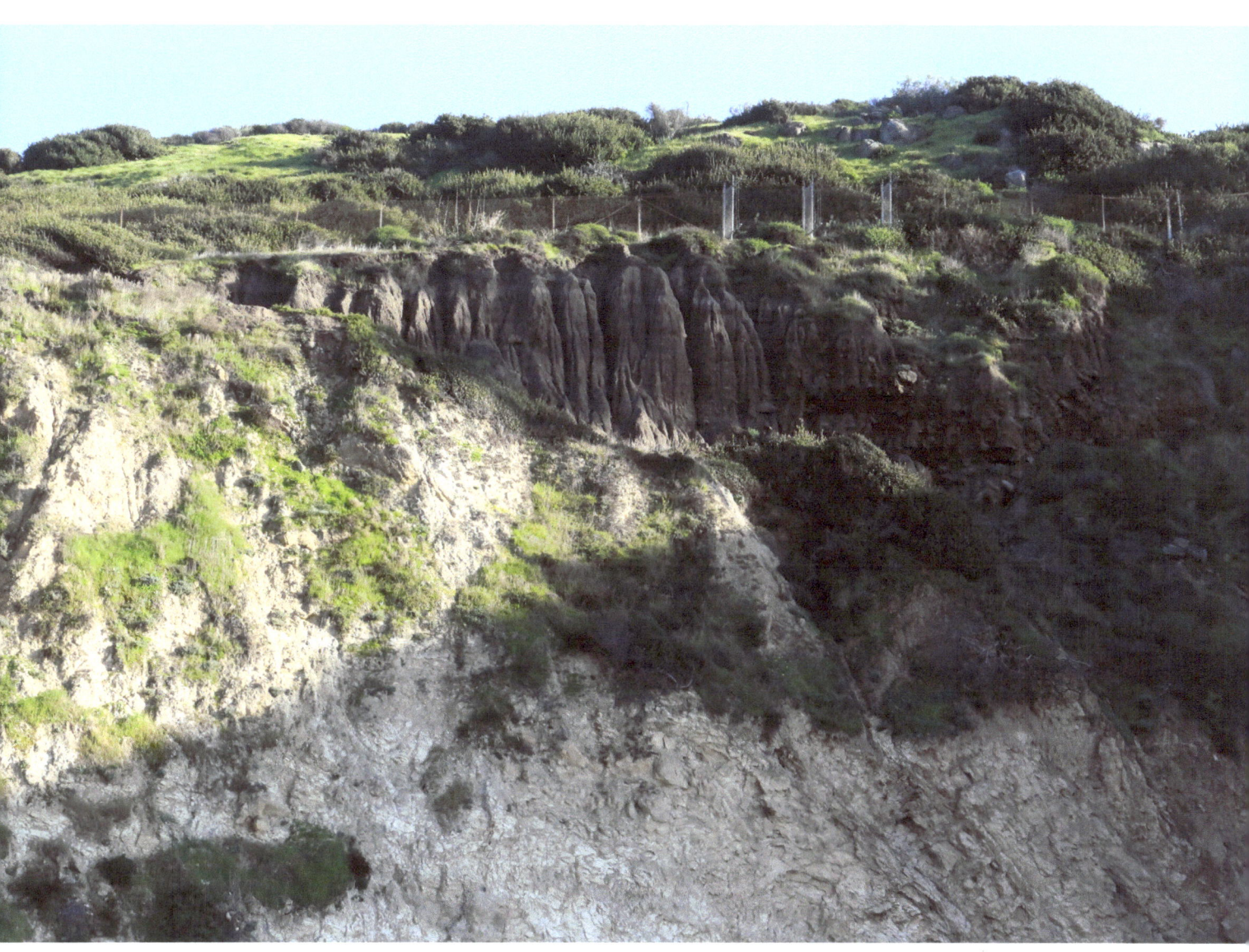

Friar Hill

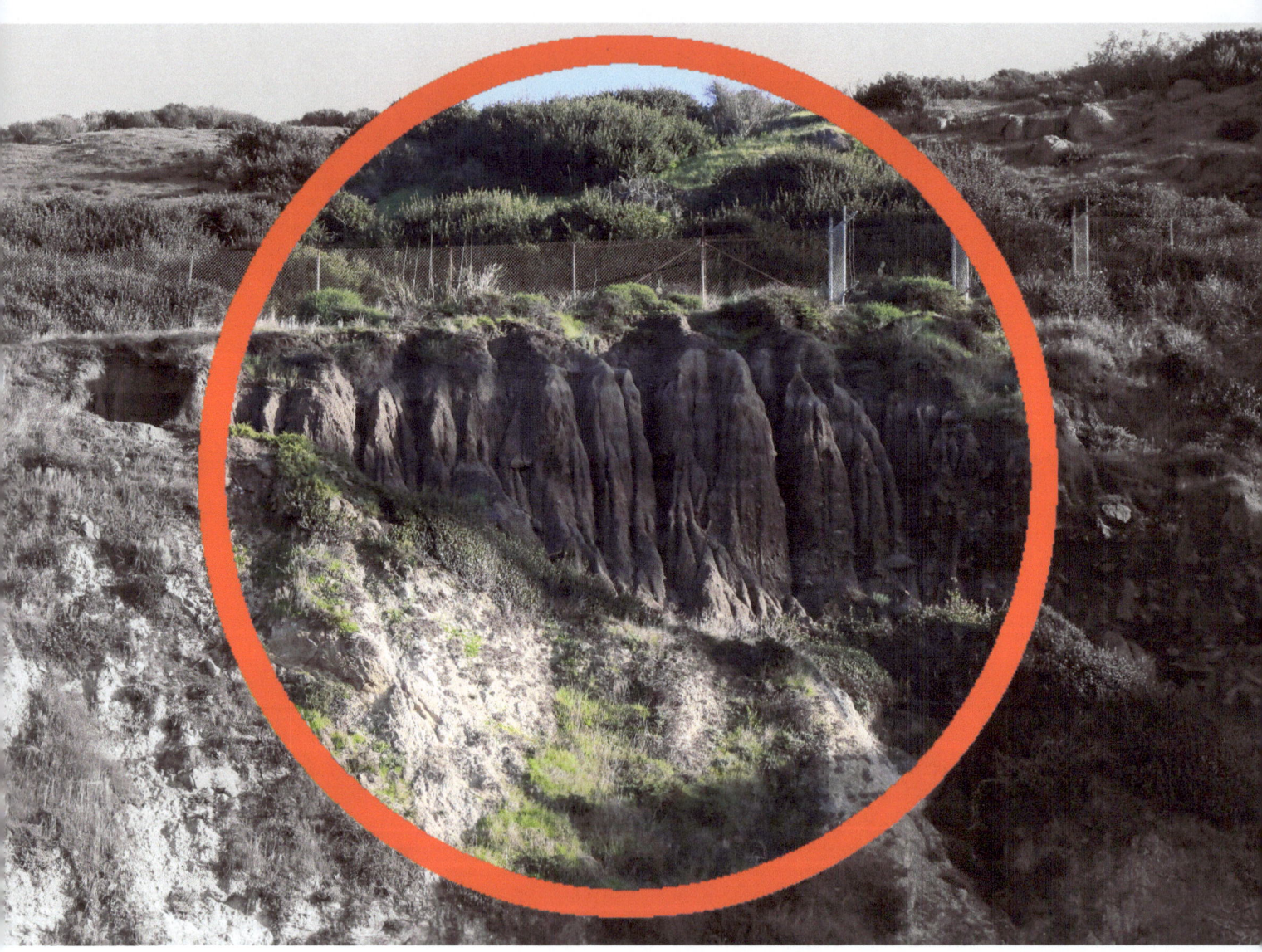

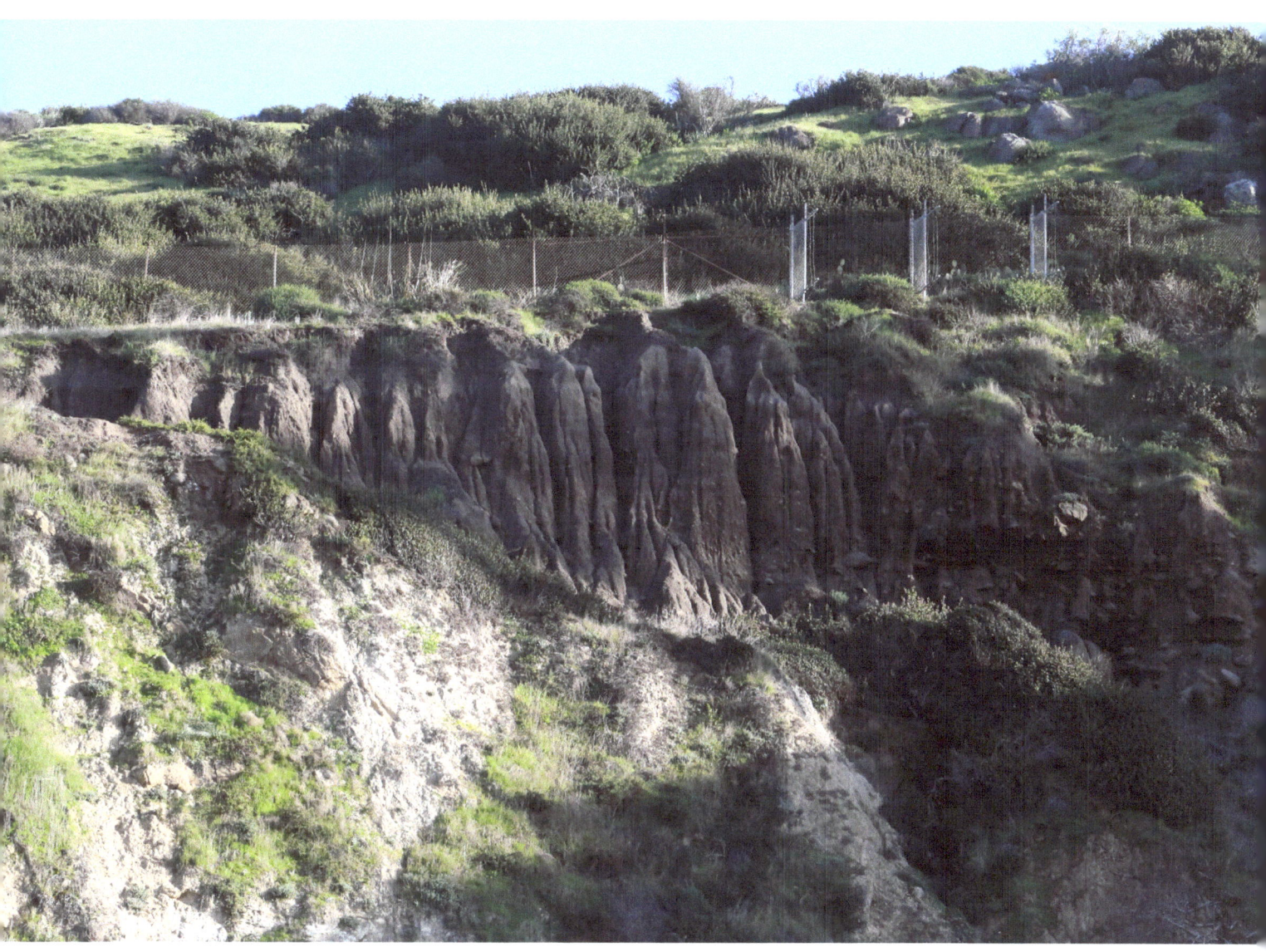

Friar Hill

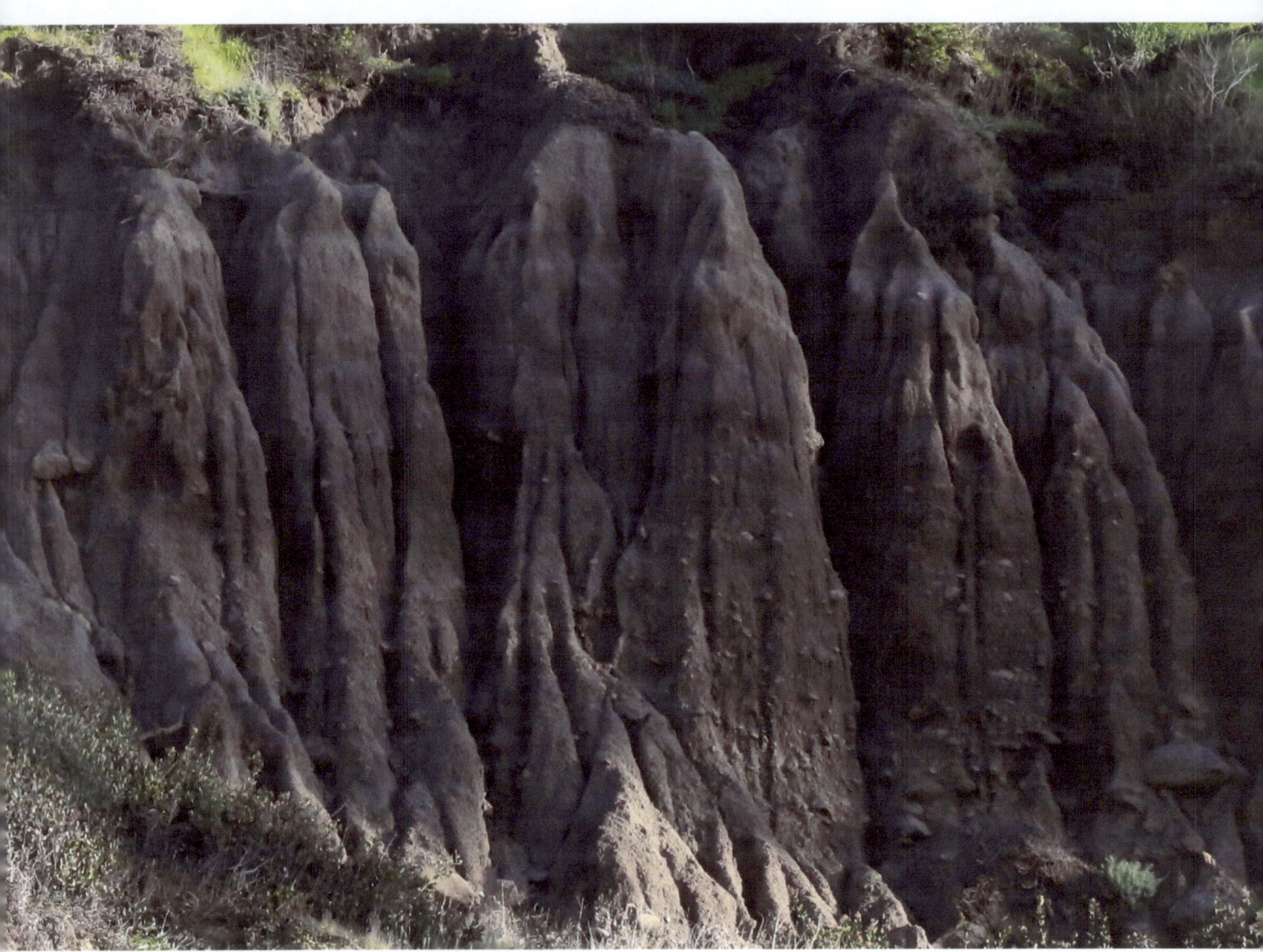

Carved by God

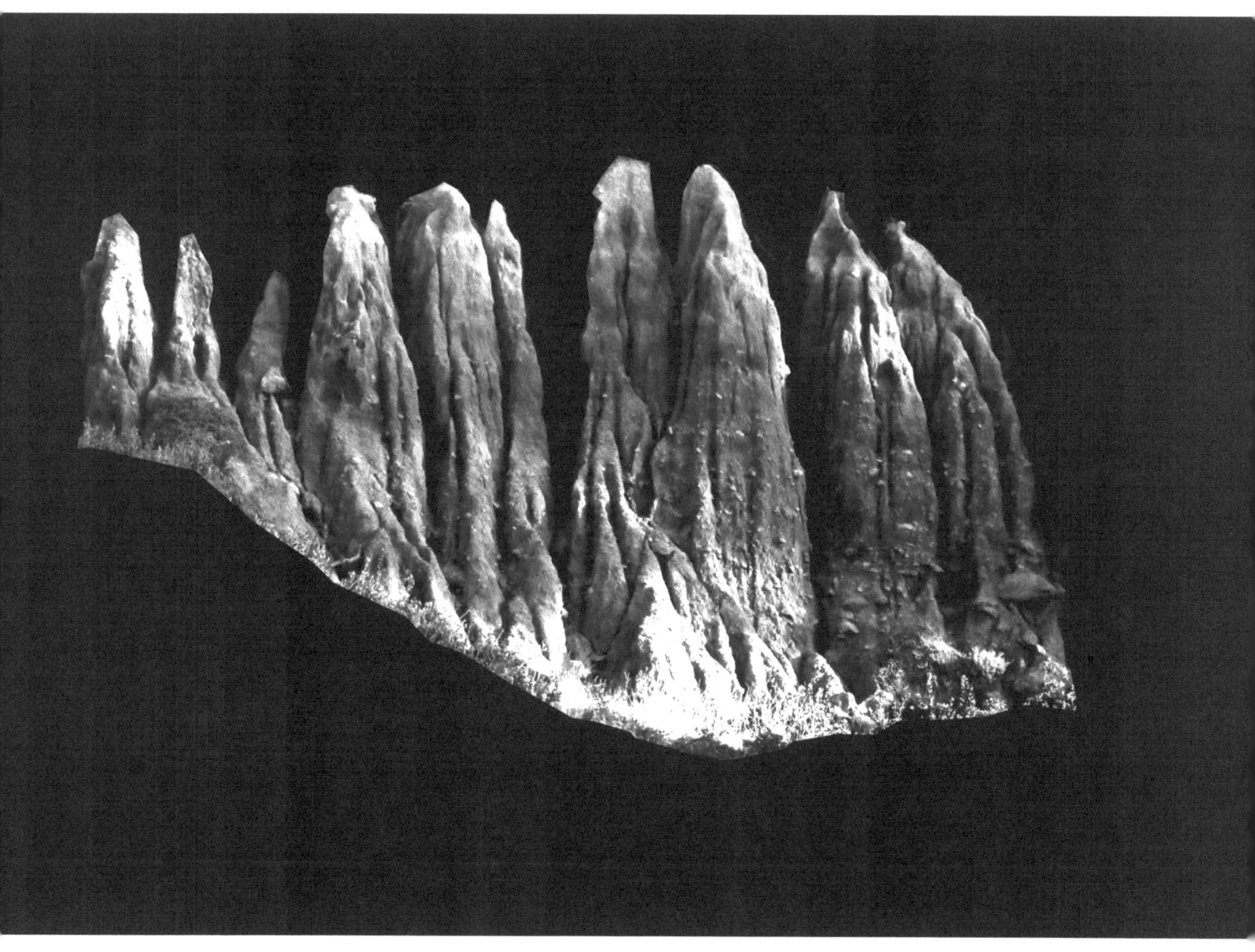

Friar Hill

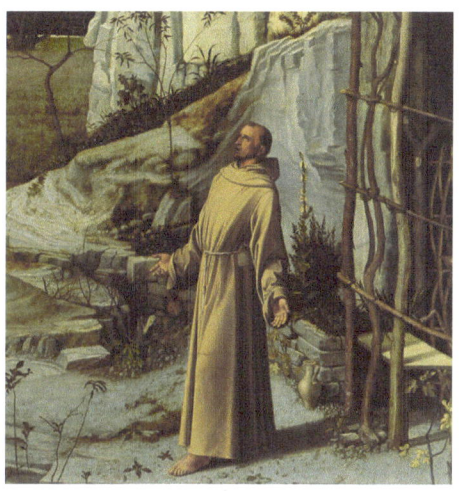

Friars in Famous Paintings

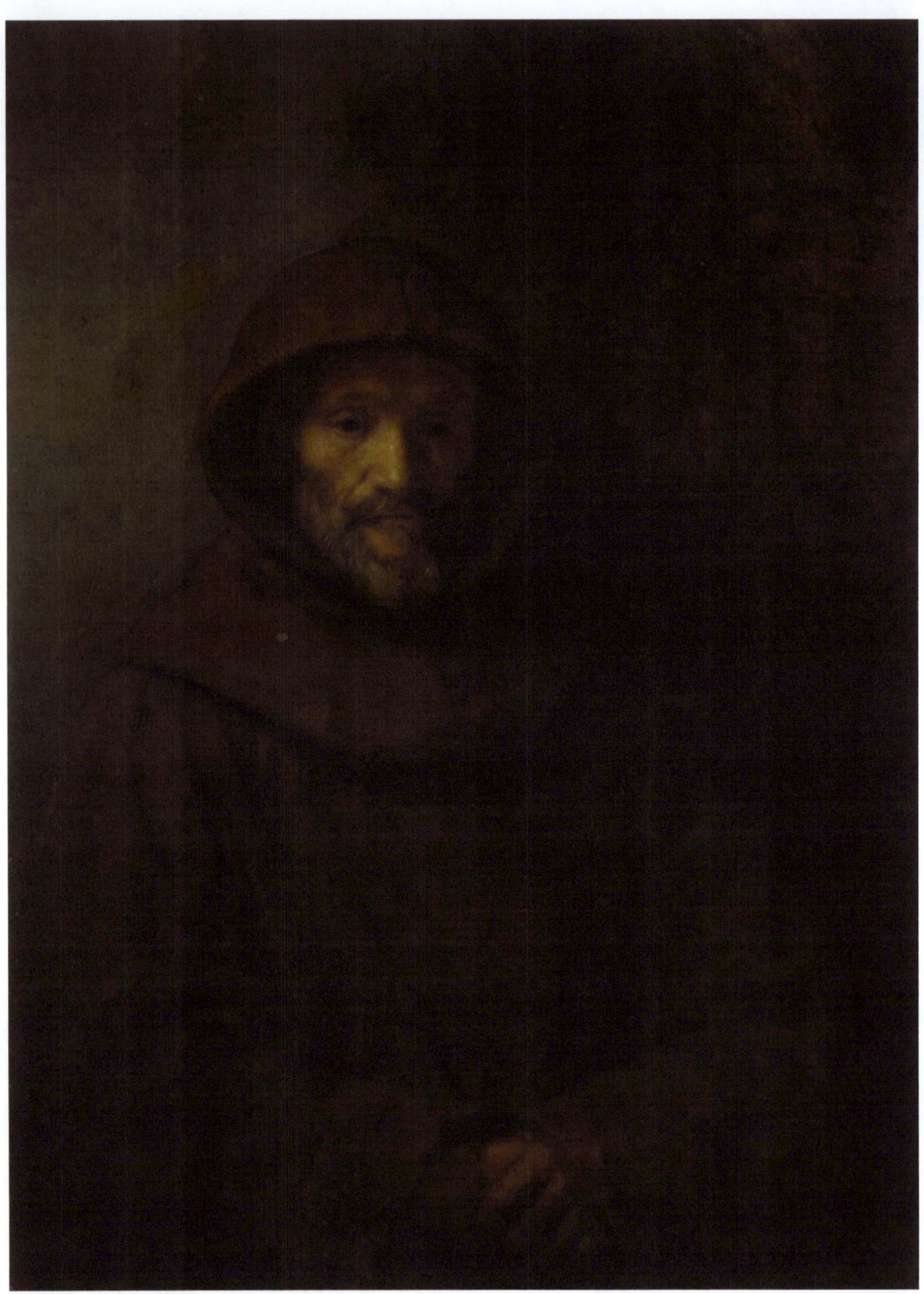

Rembrandt, *A Franciscan Friar*, 1655
The National Gallery, London

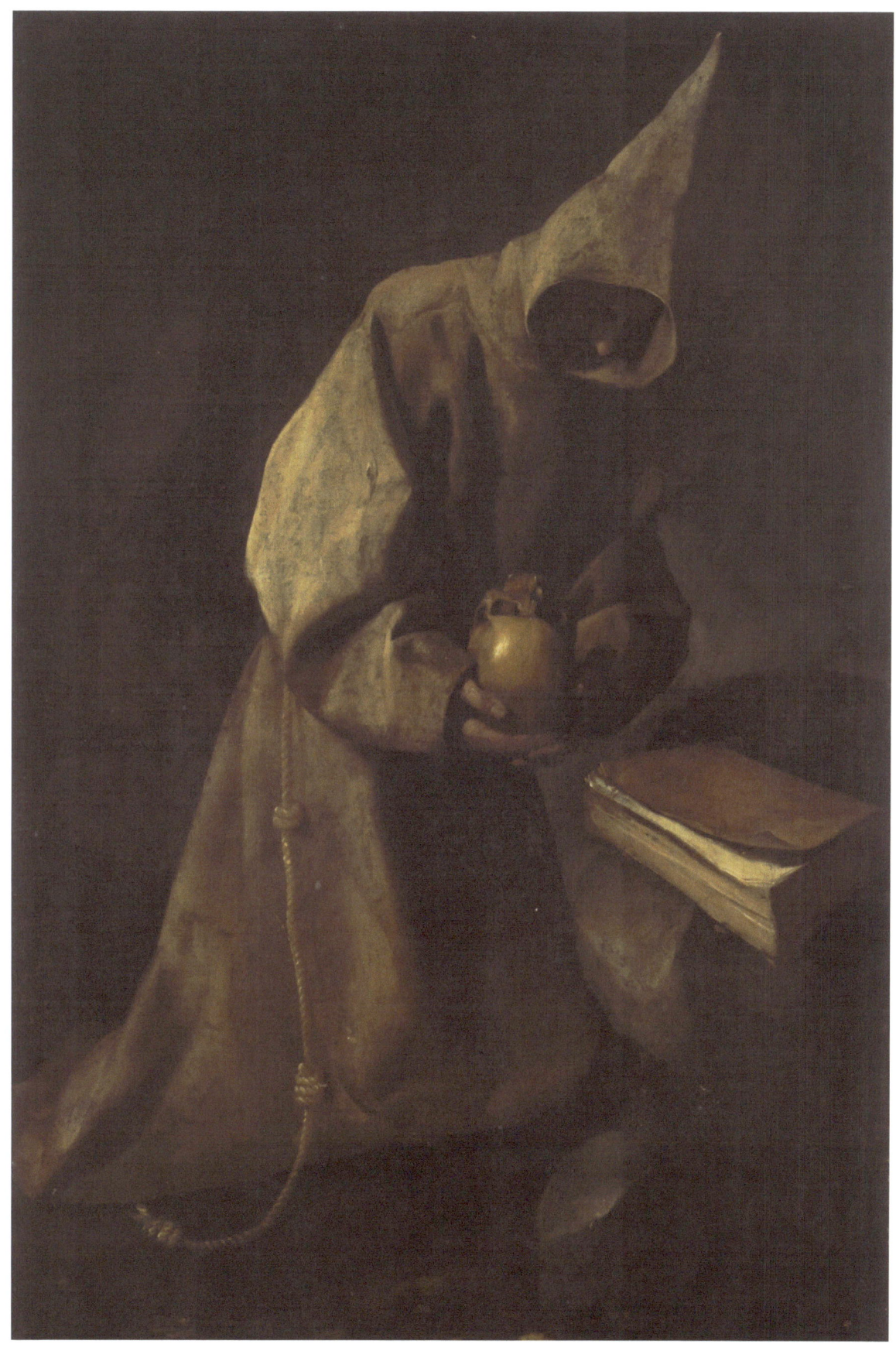

Francisco de Zurbarán, *Meditation of St Francis*, 1632
Museo Nacional de Bellas Artes, Buenos Aires

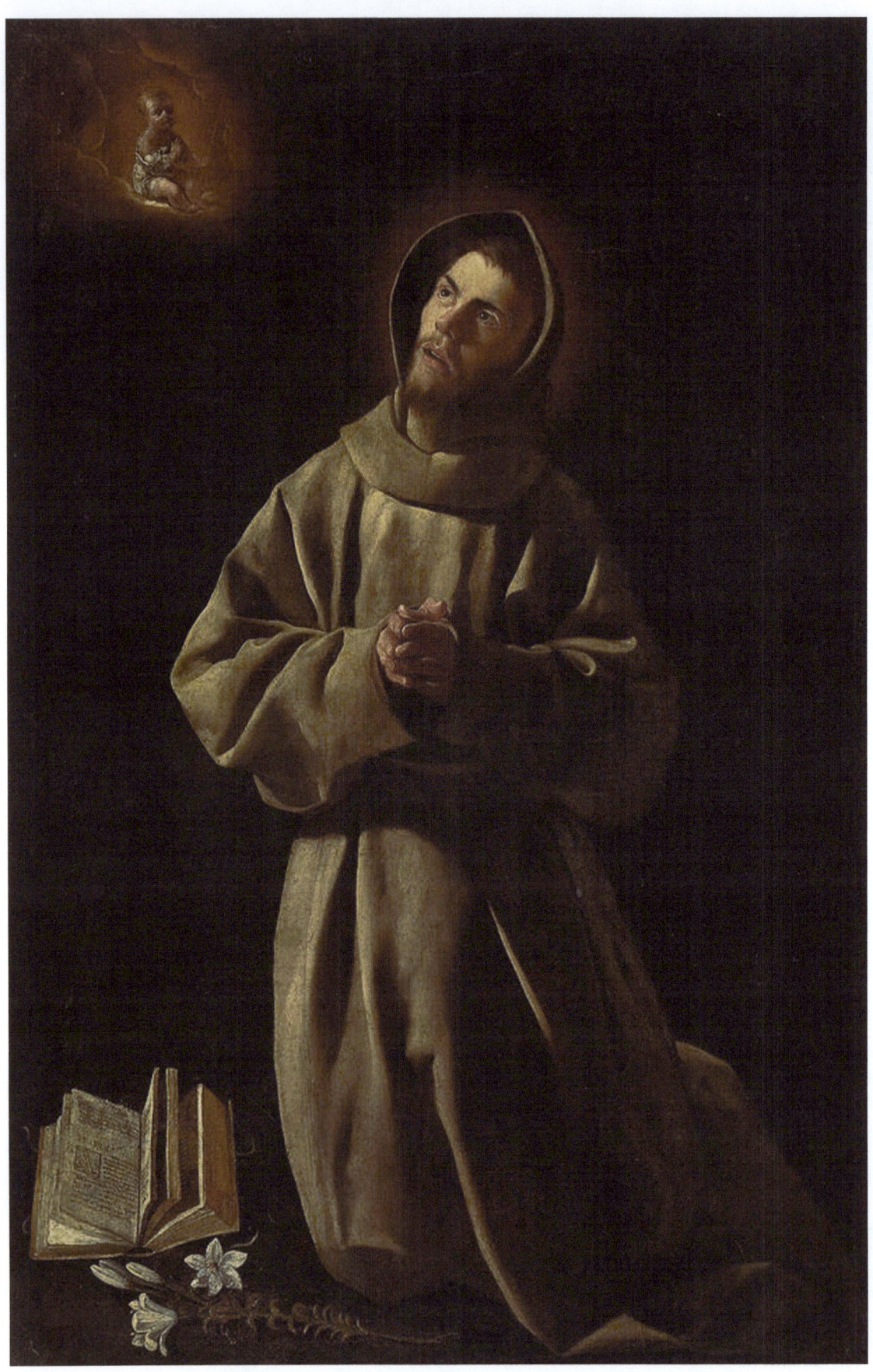

Francisco de Zurbaran, *Apparition of Jesus Child to St. Anthony of Padua*, 1627-1630
Museum of Art of São Paulo Assis Chateaubriand, São Paulo

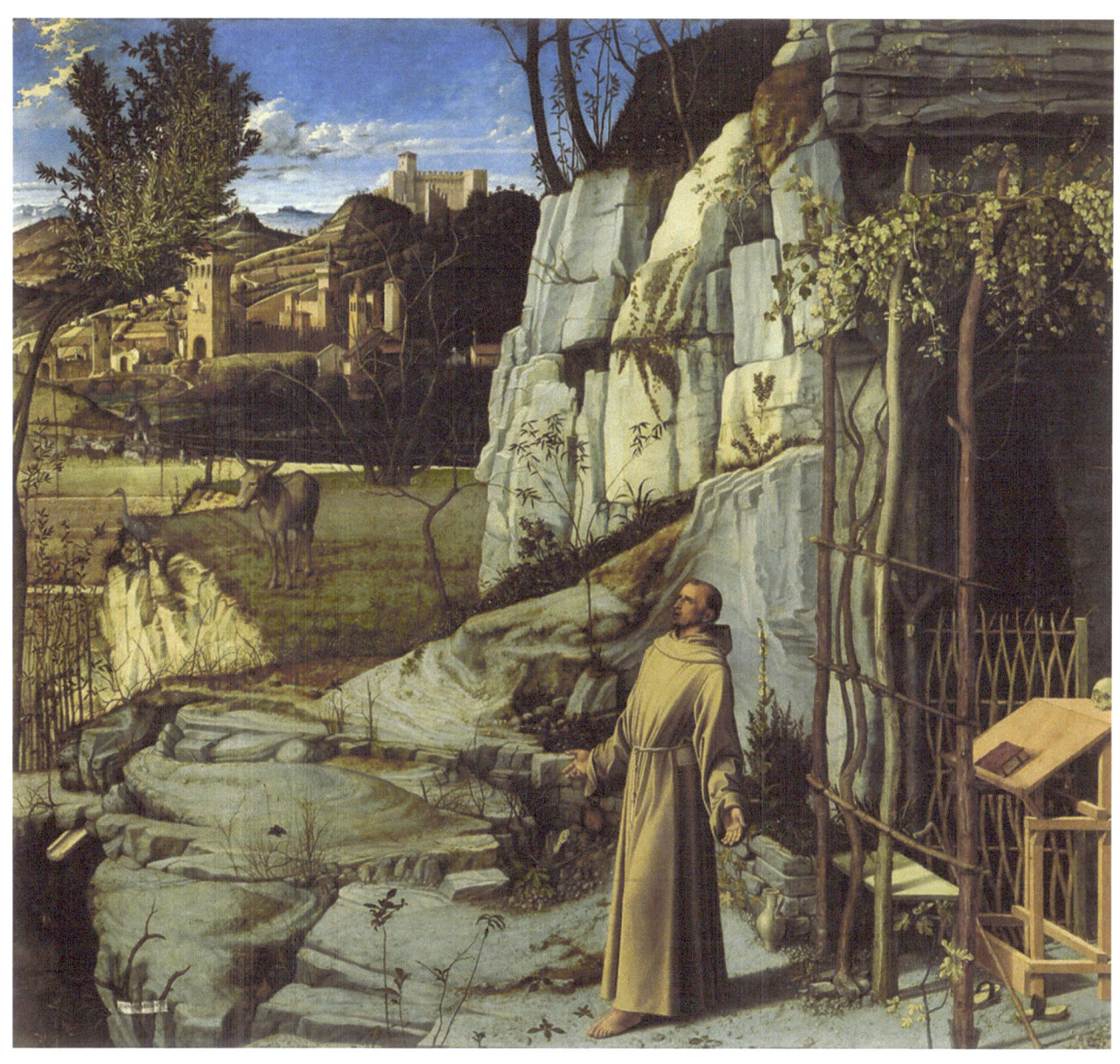

Giovanni Bellini, *St. Francis in Ecstasy*, 1480
Frick Collection, New York

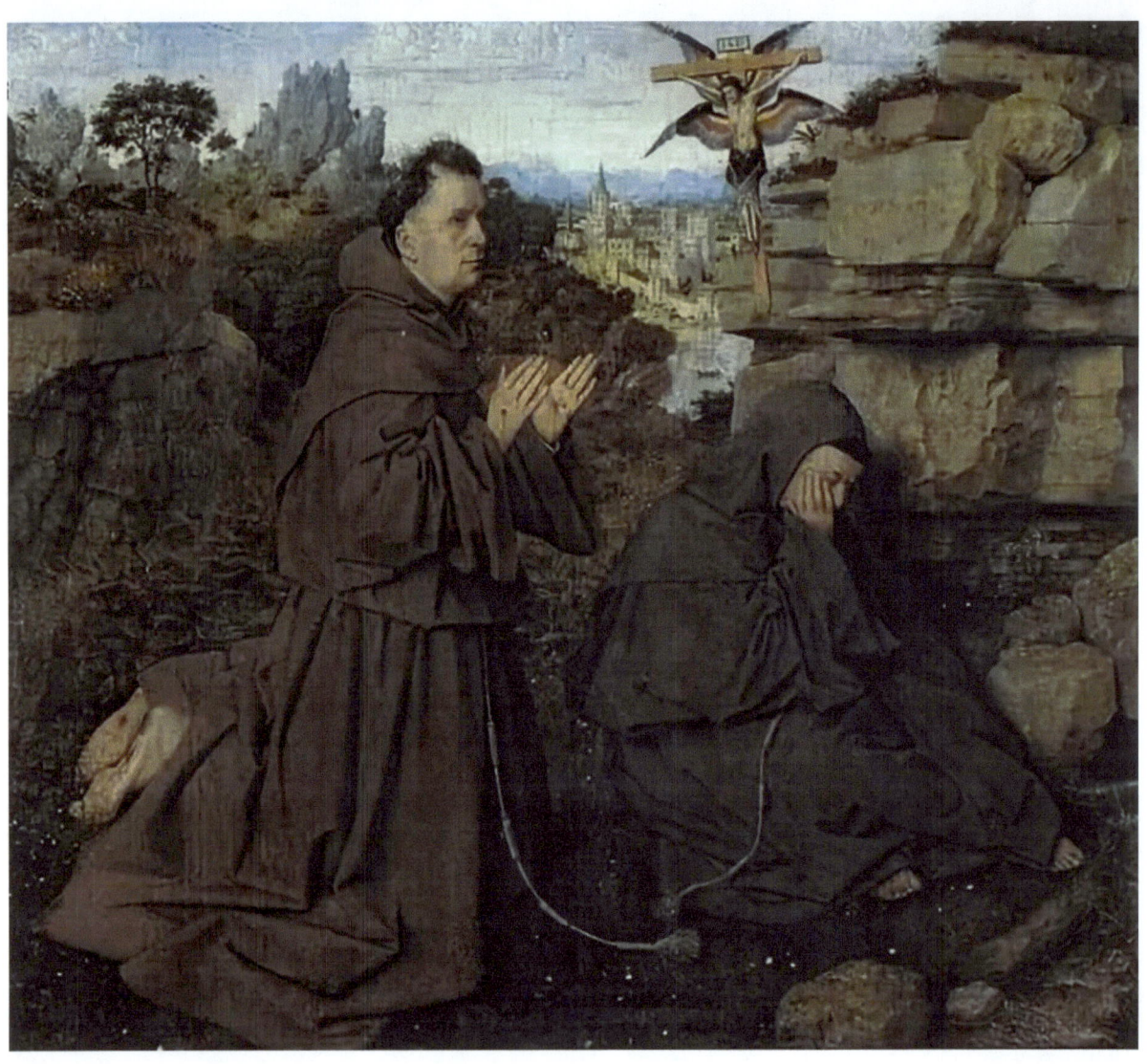

Jan van Eyck, *Saint François recevant les stigmates*, vers 1430-1432
Sabauda Gallery, Turin

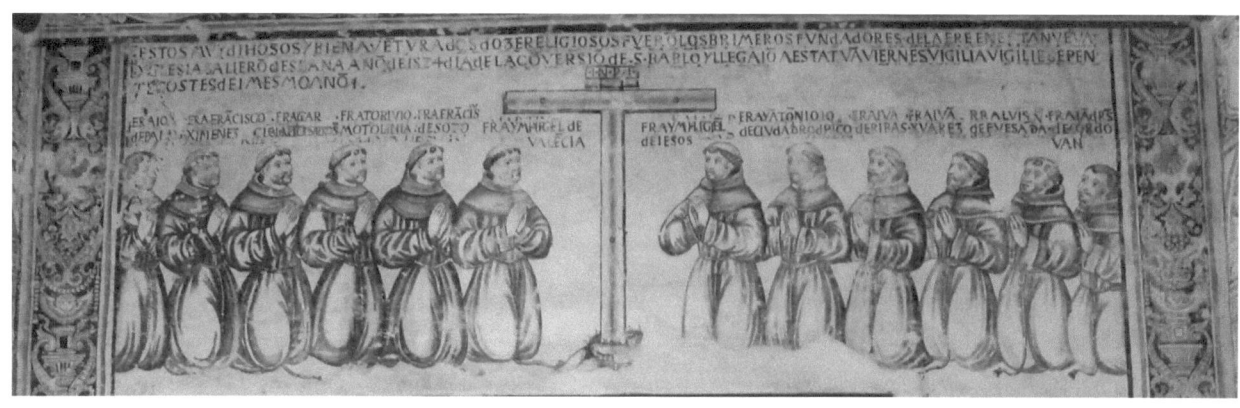

Mexico Twelve Franciscans, 16th century
Monastery of San Miguel Arcángel, Huejotzingo

Friar Hill

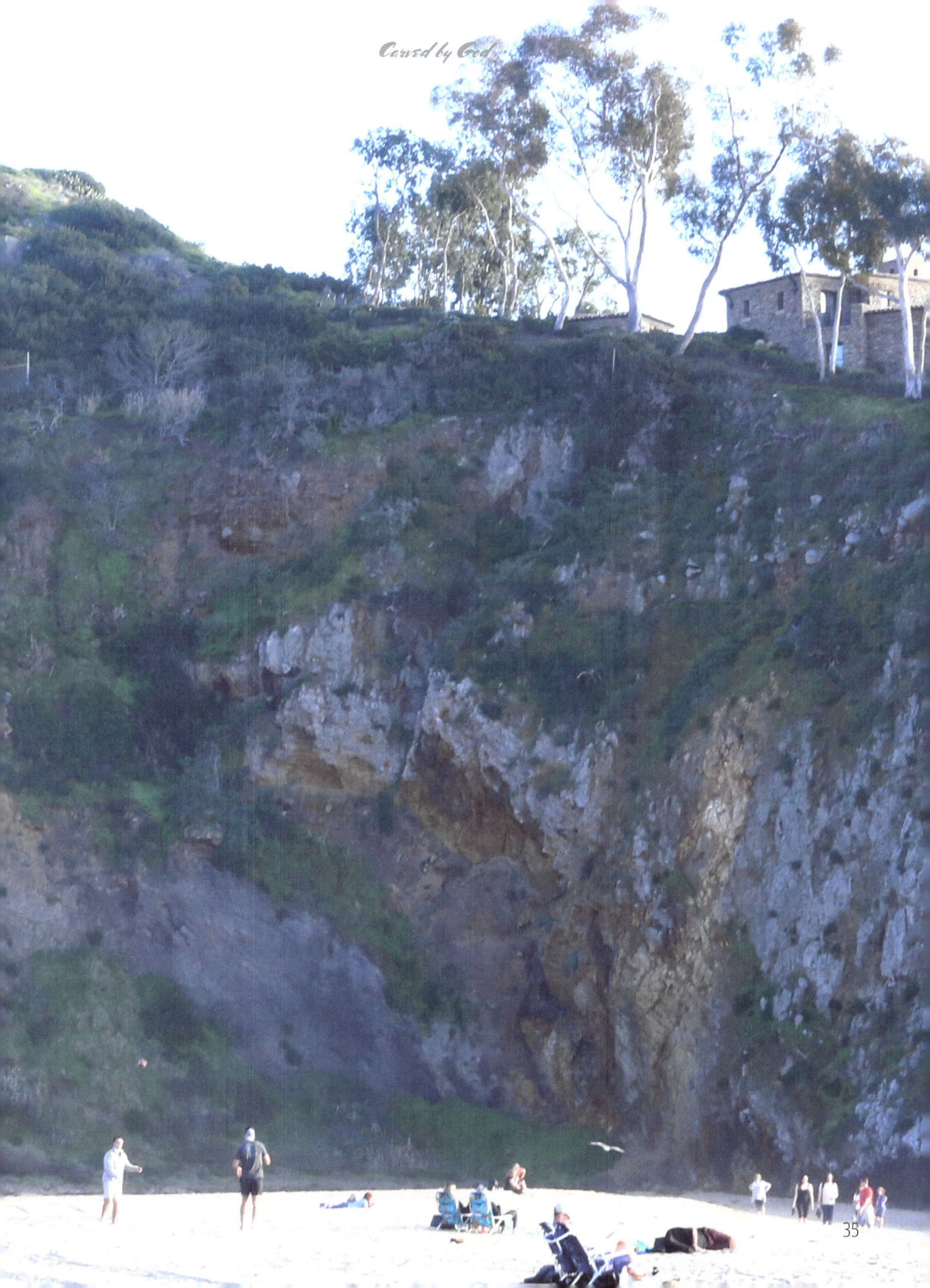

YE-MEN CHEN
Discoverer of the Natural Friar Relief

YEMEN CHEN

Illusion artist
Novelist
Chinese Homophones writer
Chinese Full-Rhymes writer
Chinese Alliterations writer

Major Works of Literature
Book of Chinese Homophones
Book of Chinese Full-Rhymes
Book of Chinese Alliterations

Major Works of Illusion Art
The Creation (2020)
Friars (2020)
Hedgehog and Deer (2016)
The Bloody Night (2016)

Achievements
Originator of "full-rhyme article".
Originator of "alliteration article".
Originator of "same-root homophone article".
Originator of "same-tone same-root homophone article".
Writer of the most homophone articles in the world.
Writer of the most full-rhyme articles in the world.
Writer of the most alliteration articles in the world.
Discoverer of natural friar statues in Friar Hill.

Records
The first "full-rhyme article" in the world.
The first "alliteration article" in the world.
The first "same-root homophone article" in the world.
The first "same-tone same-root homophone article" in the world.
The first homophones collection in the world.
The first full-rhymes collection in the world. The first alliterations collection in the world. The most homophones in the world up to now.
The most full-rhymes in the world up to now.
The most alliterations in the world up to now.
The most tongue twisters in the world up to now.

Literature Monographs
Book of Chinese Homophones (2019) Los Angeles: Losget Press.
Book of Chinese Full-Rhymes (2019) Los Angeles: Losget Press.
Book of Chinese Alliterations (2019) Los Angeles: Losget Press.
The Words of Yemen Chen (2018) Los Angeles: Losget Press.
Ballads of China (2002) Haikou: Hainan Publishing House.
Paper Tiger (2002) Haikou: Hainan Publishing House.

ONLINE BOOKSELLING

United States
https://www.amazon.com/dp/1951364015

United Kingdom
https://www.amazon.co.uk/dp/1951364015

Germany
https://www.amazon.de/dp/1951364015

France
https://www.amazon.fr/dp/1951364015

Spain
https://www.amazon.es/dp/1951364015

Italy
https://www.amazon.it/dp/1951364015

Japan
https://www.amazon.co.jp/dp/1951364015

Canada
https://www.amazon.ca/dp/1951364015

FONT DESCRIPTION

Thanks Google Open Fonts!
(https://fonts.google.com)

Amiri: Copyright 2010-2020 The Amiri Project Authors (https://github.com/alif-type/amiri).

OpenSansCondensed: Apache License Version 2.0, January 2004 http://www.apache.org/licenses/

Wallpoet: Copyright (c) 6 April 2011, Lars Berggren (lars@punktlars.se).

MrsSheppards: Copyright(c) 2011 Alejandro Paul (sudtipos@sudtipos.com).

Friar Hill

Author: Yemen Chen
Photography by Yemen Chen
Editor: Darwin Alden
Author Portrait by Jane Yu

LOSGET

Copyright © 2020 by Yemen Chen
All rights reserved.
Published in the United States by Losget Press, Los Angeles
Originally published in Paperback in the United States by
Losget Press, in 2020
Title: Friar Hill
Description: First Edition. | Los Angeles: Losget Press, 2020.
Identifiers: ISBN-13: 978-1-951364-01-4 | ISBN-10:
1-951364-01-5 | Library of Congress Control Number (LCCN):
2020934623
www.losget.com
E-mail: contact@losget.com
Book design by Yemen Chen
First Printing. 2020.

www.ingramcontent.com/pod-product-compliance
Lightning Source LLC
Chambersburg PA
CBHW051217220526
45473CB00003B/1076